MARRIAGE DESTROYERS

A Spiritual Guide to Deliverance

Dr. Davis A. Williams

Unless otherwise noted, Scripture was taken from the
NEW INTERNATIONAL VERSION BIBLE®
© Copyright 1973, 1978, 1984, 2011
Zondervan Publishers
All rights reserved. Used with permission.

Scripture quotations taken from the Amplified® Bible
© Copyright 1954, 1958, 1962, 1964, 1965, 1987 by The
Lockman Foundation.
All rights reserved. Used with permission.

ISBN   978-1-7324907-0-3
ISBN   978-1-7324907-1-0
ISBN   978-1-7324907-2-7

Marriage Destroyers: A Spiritual Guide to Deliverance.

BOOKS BY DR. DAVIS A. WILLIAMS

Altar of Addiction

Breaking the Backbone of Satan

Breaking Ancestral Curses

Altar of Infirmities

Household Wickedness

Marriage Destroyers

Silent Fire in Your Family

Be Set Free From Stagnancy

Free At Last

Heavenly Breakthroughs

Dedication

This prayer book is dedicated to the glory of Our Lord Jesus Christ, who has set me and my family free from the bondage of the kingdom of darkness to know Him, His Word, and His Ways; that everyone who prays the prayers in this book will be set free from any form of bondage, and come closer to know His glory.

To my lovely wife Prophetess Edith A. Williams, a minister of God who understands the power of prayer and unconditional love.

To God's blessings to me during good times and bad, and God's unconditional and steadfast love for me that has also allowed me to see Christ living in my family and through them, and whom I will always love and cherish; and to my children and descendants to come, each and every one.

Preface

The purpose of this book is to wage war against the kingdom of darkness, principalities, and all evil attacks. They are strictly evil.

I encourage you to use these prayers as a point of contact to be set free from the hands of the wicked.

I pray that God answers by fire. The God of Abraham, the God of Isaac, and the God of Jacob will answer your petition and allow this prayer book to be helpful and a blessing to all who use it, and that through the power of the blood of Jesus Christ that it will set you free and lead you into the cross of Calvary. To that end, this book is written.

A believer without prayer in their life is a believer without power of God within them, Jesus Christ urges us never to cease praying because the devil and his agents are always at work seeking whom they may devour.

Table of Contents

How to Save Your Marriage
from Marriage Destroyers

Introduction

Christians are a people who are always at war. Spiritual warfare is a continual battle for all believers no matter at what level of spiritual growth. Because marriage is God's illustration of the spiritual relationship between Christ and His Bride, Satan and His agents always target Christian husbands and wives for destruction. How to release your marriage from the hands of the destroyer, it is written:

> *For our struggle is not against flesh and blood, but against the rulers, against the powers, against the world forces of this darkness, against the spiritual forces of wickedness in the heavenly places. – Ephesians 6:12*
>
> *From the days of John the Baptist until now, the kingdom of heaven suffers violence, and violent men take it by force. – Matthew 11:12*

Marriage Destroyers

Have you been experiencing an issue with marriage destroyers in your marriage?

Is household wickedness taking control over your married life?

Have you been dreaming about sexual relationships while sleeping or daydreaming?

Both believers and unbelievers encounter marriage destroyers in their daily lives!

The Bible tells us in Matthew 13:25: But while his men were sleeping, his enemy came and sowed tares among the wheat, and went away.

If you are familiar with evil powers, the enemy is using your body while you sleep to expose you to sexual encounters. I urge you to seek deliverance immediately.

There are many Christians who are saved, filled with the Holy Spirit, who are also afflicted by these evil manipulations. While the Holy Spirit seals believers, believers can still *allow* evil spirits to influence their behavior. Perhaps, some do not even realize these are evil manipulations. Many of us are filled with pride, and as a result, we intend to keep this issue to ourselves rather than seek help on getting this problem resolved.

Sexual encounters through dreams are encounters with the demons Incubus and Succubus, or *spirit husband* and *spirit wife.* Sexual experiences with demonic spirits are real. If you have been experiencing a problem of sexual encounters in your dreams, this is very common. It is evil manipulation driven by demonic powers.

Incubus: These evil spirits lie upon sleeping persons – especially women – with whom it seeks sexual intercourse. Demonic sexual attacks on females may be caused by sexual sins, witchcraft spells, and curses of lust, inherited curses, or being a victim of sexual abuse. Succubus: Evil spirits that seduce sleeping persons – especially men – work the same way.

Unfortunately, there are many parents who abuse their children sexually. A powerful evil spirit called the spirit of Sexual Perversion is controlling them. These evil spells and curses on parents control their abusive behavior, causing them to abuse their daughter or son repeatedly, and to have sexual intercourse with them against the children's will. It is not consensual sex, no matter how the parent may try to deceive himself or herself. Most of these parents are filled with the violent evil spirits because of spells and curses. These evil spirits are controlling their lives today.

The Bible tells us in Genesis 12:3:

And I will bless those who bless you,

And the one who curses you I will curse.

And in you all the families of the earth will be blessed.

There are also many men and women that have been spiritually isolated, blocked, or chained down by evil spirits. This is oppression. As a result, it has been very difficult for husband and wife to remain physically married. Frustrations and disappointments dominate in their marriage because the evil spiritual spouses dictate reactions to marital situations. They block healthy relationships between husband and wife.

These spirit husbands and wives are jealous and do not want anyone to come between their marriages – meaning if you are single or married and notice that you have been experiencing sexual intercourse constantly in your dreams or daydreams, you have been married in the spiritual realm with these violent evil spirits called Incubus and Succubus—also known as spirit husband and spirit wife. These violent spirits intend to block many single individuals from earthly marriage. If you are married, these violent evil spirits start intervening in your affairs, meaning these spirits have forcefully taken you in the spiritual realm, and you belong to them, therefore, they control your sex life. Your earthly husband or wife has no more control over your sex life.

If you have been a victim of any evil spirit, a solution to your problem is deliverance through spiritual warfare prayer. Also, you should consult with your minister for deliverance. Regardless, you should follow these prayer instructions carefully for a spiritual warfare self-deliverance, and let God be God in your life.

Pray these prayers sincerely with the Bible passages.

Confession: Psalm 7:17, John 5:14, 1 Corinthians 3:16

I will give thanks to the Lord according to His Righteousness
And will sing praise to the name of the Lord Most High.

– Psalm 7:17

Afterward Jesus found him in the temple and said to him, "Behold, you have become well; do not sin anymore, so that nothing worse happens to you." – John 5:14

Do you not know that you are a temple of God and that the Spirit of God dwells in you? – 1 Corinthians 3:16

You will become proficient at praying God's will into your life. Using Scripture to pray is always praying God's will because it is His Word you are speaking into your life. Many people are not familiar with warfare prayers, or how to wage war during spiritual attacks. With this prayer book, after going through the entire spiritual exercises, you will be better attuned to God's will, and He will fill your spiritual needs with better results.

Pray with persistence until you receive a successful result. Do not give up when the evil spirits resist you, and they will. You will do well by following the principles in the Holy Bible and how to pray effective prayers with answers to prayer.

The prayers in this book follow Scripture, and target specific needs *one at a time.* Each prayer request must complete the whole twenty-one-day time period before proceeding to the next prayer request. *Fasting is optional.* Utilizing the full three-week time period is crucial because fighting a spiritual battle requires serious praying and fasting. Not everyone is able to fast for medical or other reasons, therefore praying for the full twenty-one days is essential. In theory, any constant prayer after three days in the same petition one must experience results on such petition. The majority of the people that I pray over for deliverance, or they pray the deliverance prayer for three to seven days, start seeing the changes in their behavior. Don't make the mistake of letting up on your prayer time.

Since many people are not strong in their spiritual life and cannot fast, I recommend for those to try and finish the whole twenty-one days' prayer chain. You will stand a stronger chance these evil spirits will leave you completely.

In spiritual warfare, most of the issues we fight against trying to free ourselves from our evil manipulations are generational curses that transfer from generation to generation. Some of these evil spirits are very stubborn, meaning they are very comfortable with you therefore praying to set yourself free from them, is not going to be an easy battle. So, when you repeatedly pray these prayers under a scheduled time frame, it forces them to let go and leave you alone. In my research, I found it more efficient to pray for twenty-one days to be completely set free.

Special Instructions:
1. Locate your area of need by looking at the table of contents.
2. Select appropriate scriptures promising you what you desire.
3. Meditate on these and let the Holy Spirit do the rest.
4. Twenty-one days of consistent and constant prayer: 12 a.m., 6 a.m., 12 p.m., and 6 p.m.

Of all the times for your prayers during your spiritual battle, the most critical time is at 12:00 A.M. It is mandatory to pray this prayer for a spiritual battle. After that, one can pray anytime during the day.

I selected these particular hours for us to get used to the actual prayer schedule like a fasting schedule. Therefore, in the future, if you encounter any other issues, you will not need to consult a minister, but instead you can wage war for yourself and even intercede for your spouse and family.

Pray in the Spirit, and let the good Lord take control of your situation.

> *And without faith, it is impossible to please Him, for he who comes to God must believe that He is and that He is a rewarder of those who seek Him.* – Hebrews 11:6

Life is a battle, and we are all born into a battlefield. We should always be ready to fight the evil spirits, and destroy their influence over our lives since their assignment is to kill and destroy us.

Beloved, your prayer petitions help you to align yourself to God's perfect will. They help you recognize the sin for what it is, and that helps you to resist the temptations. Hopefully, you will get a better understanding of how to develop a closer relationship with God while you pray by understanding how prayer works in your daily living.

The evil spirits that may bind us have names that include:

- Pornography
- Fornication
- Masturbation
- Sexual Perversion
- Prostitution
- Polygamy
- Gender Confusion
- Bestiality
- Rape
- Spirit of Jezebel
- Anger
- Bitterness
- Murder
- Theft
- Witchcraft
- Divorce
- Depression
- Bondage

Their purposes include demonic attacks, spirit husband and spirit wife attacks, sexual relationships in dreams, marriage killers, abusive actions such as verbal abuse and physical abuse, divorce, deep depression, evil children, marital oppression, destroying marriages, evil blood covenants, marital bondage, curses, devouring good judgment concerning finances and, spirit of barrenness (no spiritual fruit or physical fruit). Recognize these for what they are.

Therefore, after finishing the desired section of your prayer petition, you must command the evil spirits to leave you. Voice out loud whatever situations you recognize you are in, "I renounce you and all your works in my life! I command you in the mighty name of Jesus Christ to lose your grip and release me now by the thunder fire of God!"

You may have to continue to rebuke them in the mighty name of Jesus Christ, and command the spirits to leave since demons can often be very aggressive and stubborn. But if you continue to rebuke them for seven times, by the power of the blood of Jesus Christ, they will leave you in Jesus' name.

While rebuking the demons, you may feel like you want to throw up, cough, sneeze, yawn deeply, or scream. These reactions are normal—no need to be alarmed. All legions, demons, and the satanic agents often manifest in such a manner while leaving your body.

How can one know that they have left one's body? You will feel a sense of relief, or you will no longer feel so sensitive to the attacks you faced before the deliverance. After the spirits are gone, such evil attacks that were controlling your life will diminish, and you will see a wonderful change in your life.

So how do you retain your deliverance? Many of these demonic forces will leave you after the deliverance, but will patiently watch and wait at a distance eager to snatch you back into their clutches. Bear in mind that expelling the legions and demons are just stage one of your deliverance. To maintain your deliverance, you will need to start changing your lifestyle by renewing your mind with the word of the Lord.

> *Therefore, I urge you, brethren, by the mercies of God, to present your bodies a living and holy sacrifice, acceptable to God, which is your spiritual service of worship. And do not be conformed to this world, but be transformed by the renewing of your mind, so that you may prove what the will of God is, that which is good and acceptable and perfect.*

> *– Romans 12:1-2*

Engage yourself with the activities of the Lord, so that you will always remain in the presence of the Lord, as Satan and his agents are always looking for an opportunity to draw you back into the kingdom of darkness, to hold you in bondage again because of your ungodly behavior acting upon ungodly thoughts. Of course, you can fill your mind with God's word, and not dwell upon evil thoughts that flit into your mind. These demons will do anything to make you turn your face away from God. Therefore,

> Put on the full armor of God, so that you will be able to stand firm against the schemes of the devil. For our struggle is not against flesh and blood, but against the rulers, against the powers, against the world forces of this darkness, against the spiritual forces of wickedness in the heavenly places.

> – Ephesians 6:11-12

It is very important for you not to give any chance to Satan and his agents. You must keep reading the word of the Lord, and pray with it daily by the power of the blood of Jesus Christ, or your life will never be safe from demonic attacks.

You will win the battle in Jesus' name. Amen.

The Bible tells us in Ephesians 6:12:

> For our struggle is not against flesh and blood, but against the rulers, against the powers, against the world forces of this darkness, against the spiritual forces of wickedness in the heavenly places.

NOTE: The prayers are *not* directed against human beings. We Christians do *not* fight against flesh and blood. Understand the attack is coming from parents, siblings, in-laws, relatives, past relationships, or from friends, but invisible forces carry out the evil assignment to destroy your marriage; these are unseen spirits from the kingdom of darkness. What we see from the human perspective is the instrument that Satan and his agents use on earth to destroy many good things in our lives.

Chapter 1

Prayer of Thanksgiving

Praise the Lord!

Praise God in His sanctuary;

Praise Him in His mighty expanse.

Praise Him for His mighty deeds;

Praise Him according to His excellent greatness.

Praise Him with trumpet sound,

Praise Him with harp and lyre.

Praise Him with timbrel and dancing;

Praise Him with stringed instruments and pipe.

Praise Him with loud cymbals;

Praise Him with resounding cymbals.

Let everything that has breath praise the Lord.

Praise the Lord! - Psalm 150:1-6:

AMEN.

Daily Thanksgiving

Praises and Worship

Christian Songs of Your Choice

1. Thank You Jesus, thank You, my Lord…
2. You are Alpha and Omega that we worship, You are Lord…
3. Covenant keeping God there is no one like You…

Beloved God Almighty, our creator, has done many things in our lives.

Why is it difficult for us to open our mouth and thank Him for the many things He has done for us? Let's look back in our lives and see how far the good Lord has brought us … Many of us shouldn't have been alive but by His grace and mercy, we are still alive. We should be thankful!

Some complain:

I have nothing to be thankful about.

God hasn't really done anything for me to be thankful for...

I submit to you that God *has* done a lot for us to be thankful for; the air we breathe alone is enough for us to be thankful.

Let's start thanking Him for the many things He has done for us.

Now therefore, our God, we thank You, and praise Your glorious name. – 1 Chronicles 29:13

I shall give thanks to You, for You have answered me, And You have become my salvation. – Psalm 118:21

Prayer

God of Abraham, Isaac, and Jacob: Your name is Jehovah. You are the Alpha and Omega. There is no one like You. Heavenly Father, I glorify Your mighty name, Jehovah Lord. You are the Omnipresent God, the Omnipotent God, the Father of the Fatherless. It is not Your will that I should perish, but I might have repentance.

Everlasting Father, Your, blood makes sinners clean. Heavenly Father, have mercy on me. Wash me truly from my iniquities, and cleanse me from my sins; sanctify me with the blood of Jesus Christ.

Lord Jesus, save my marriage from the hands of the wicked. Everlasting Redeemer, destroy every evil network against my marriage. Heavenly Father, wherever they have gathered against me, against my marriage, against my carrier, against my finances, in their coven, I commend them to receive the thunder fire of God in Jesus' name.

God that answers by fire, I command their entire works — their plans, and magical mirror which they are using to monitor and control my life, my marriage, my carrier, and my finances — to be destroyed in Jesus' name.

Heavenly Father, You, are the healer, Your, word tells us that by Your stripes we shall be healed. Father Lord, I agreed upon Your word. Heal every department in my life, heal every broken area in my marriage, Everlasting Redeemer, heal me where I need healing, transform me where I need transformation, and deliver me where I need deliverance in the matchless name of Jesus Christ.

1. Father Lord, I thank You for Your divine favor upon my life.
2. Father Lord, I thank You for Your divine blessings upon my life.
3. Father Lord, I thank You for Your divine salvation upon my life.
4. Father Lord, I thank You for making impossible things possible in my life.
5. Father Lord, I thank You for giving me the power of the fear of the Lord.
6. Father Lord, I thank You for helping me to overcome my unbelief's.
7. Father Lord, I thank You for looking over me.
8. Father Lord, I thank You for the breath You have given me.
9. Father Lord, I thank You for making a way for me, where there is no way.
10. Father Lord, I thank You for Your Holy Spirit upon my life.
11. Father Lord, I thank You for guiding my path day in and day out.
12. Father Lord, I thank You for being my provider.
13. Father Lord, I thank You for baptizing me with the Holy Spirit.
14. Father Lord, I thank You for Your angels guiding me.
15. Father Lord, I thank You for allowing the fear of the Lord to dwell in me.
16. Father Lord, I thank You for keeping me in perfect peace.
17. Father Lord, I thank You for intervening in my affairs.
18. Father Lord, I thank You for Your divine purpose and plans over my life.

19. Father Lord, I thank You for Your divine joy and peace upon my life.
20. Father Lord, I thank You for accepting me into Your kingdom as I am.
21. Father Lord, I thank You for looking over me while sleeping.
22. Father Lord, I thank You for healing my body, soul, and mind.
23. Father Lord, I thank You for Your power, glory, and righteousness upon my life.
24. Father Lord, I thank You for delivering me from the hands of the wicked.
25. Father Lord, I thank You for delivering my family from the hands of the   strongmen.
26. Father Lord, I thank You for not allowing my adversaries to rejoice over me.
27. Father Lord, I thank You for Your divine protection upon my family.
28. Father Lord, I thank You for Your angels looking over me.
29. Father Lord, I thank You for Your greatness and splendor.
30. Father Lord, I thank You for silencing the foe and my adversaries.
31. Father Lord, I thank You for Your faithfulness and marvelous deeds.
32. Father Lord, I thank You for being my God, in Jesus' name. Amen.

Chapter 2

Prayers of Forgiveness

Prayers

Father Lord, I am a sinner with unclean lips, Lord Jesus have mercy upon me. Everlasting Father, Everlasting Redeemer, any sin in my life that would hinder my prayer of getting answered today, Lord Jesus, forgive me.

Anyone I have sinned against that I do not know about, Lord Jesus, forgive me in Jesus' name.

Heavenly Father, Your, word declares it in Isaiah 54:17: No weapon that is formed against You will prosper; every tongue that accuses You in judgment You will condemn. "This is the heritage of the servants of the Lord, and their vindication is from Me," declares the Lord.

Lord Jesus, I come against every principality assigned to wreck my marriage, in Jesus' name.

I am in agreement with Matthew 18:18, and bind every evil activity here on Earth against my marriage, so it is bound in Heaven. You, powers of the night against my marriage, I rebuke you in Jesus' name.

Heavenly Father, Everlasting Redeemer, and the Most High God, based on Your eternal word of God, I command all principalities, wizards, witches, marine spirit, and evil priests chanting my name for evil to be consumed by the mighty fire of God.

Any ungodly spirit, anyone undergoing fasting against my life, my family, and my marriage should perish in Jesus' name.

God that answers by fire, Eternal Rock of Ages, put the devil to shame. Father Lord, set the captive free from all evil bondage.

Jehovah Lord, I dedicate my marriage unto You to hold down the foundation as a solid rock; my family and I are set free from the dominion of the kingdom of darkness. I shield my marriage with the precious blood of Jesus Christ. Amen.

1. Any power secretly stealing good things from my life, your time has expired; perish now in Jesus' name.
2. Lord Jesus, let their way be dark and slippery, and let the angel of the Lord persecutes, them in the mighty name of Jesus. For without cause, have they hid for me their net in a pit, which without cause, they have dug for my soul.
3. Let destruction come upon him unaware, and let his net that he has hidden catch himself; let him fall into that destruction he designed for me in Jesus' name.
4. Father Lord, I reject every evil family ancestral name.
5. I break the power of any evil dedication ever placed on my head, every pledge, vow, promise, or covenant ever made on my behalf with these spirits; I renounce them, and reject them cutting myself off from them with the blood of Jesus from all their evil consequences.
6. I soak myself in the blood of Jesus.
7. I soak myself in the blood of Jesus.
8. I soak myself in the blood of Jesus.
9. I cover my family with the blood of Jesus Christ.
10. I cover my home with the blood of Jesus Christ.
11. My life, I anchor to the promises of my Heavenly Father to be fruitful in Jesus' name.
12. The blood of Jesus shall seal any evil door opened in my life.
13. Convert failure in my life to success in Jesus' name.
14. Oh Lord, help me not to be afraid to move forward in Jesus' name.

15. The battle of impiety shall not catch up with me in the name of Jesus.

16. In Jesus' name, Thou, ancient of days, the great I Am that I am, the beginning and the end, the Eternal Rock of Ages, Thou God of Abraham, Isaac and Jacob, from everlasting to everlasting You are God, Father Lord, as I mention Your name, every knee must bow. Lord Jesus, receive all my thanks in Jesus' name, Father Lord. I bow down my knees before You this moment. Through Your strength, I stand against any soul that is against this prayer, I command in the name of the Father, in the name of the son, and the Holy Spirit, let that soul receive fire of God, in Jesus' name.

17. Lord Jesus have mercy upon me. Lord, save me from witches and wizards, save my family from witches and wizards, save my parents from witches and wizards, save my home from witches and wizards, in the name of Jesus Christ.

18. I use the blood of Jesus to cleanse myself, and I cover my home, my properties, my family, and my friends with the blood of Jesus Christ.

19. Every curse that is against me from my forefathers, I have nullified them by the blood of Jesus Christ. Every curse from every evil agent – from my father's family, from my mother's family – is destroyed in Jesus' name.

20. Lord, I thank You for Your grace and power that has protected me and my family, in the matchless name of Christ Jesus.

21. Father Lord, I claim all my blessings from the hands of the destroyer. I stand inside Your authority against any spirit of disappointment, and the spirit of hatred in my life, also in the lives of the members in my family. In Jesus' name, be destroyed.

22. Father Lord, whenever the agent of darkness joins hands against me scatter them by Your fire in Jesus' name.

23. The Father of the Fatherless shall be my Father in Jesus' name.
24. Lord, make disgrace and defeat depart as evil strangers in my life.
25. Lord, make my case be too hot for them to handle in Jesus' name.
26. Lord, destroy any power delegated to monitor me for evil, in Jesus' name.
27. Thou, who gave favor to Joseph, favor me in Jesus' name.
28. Lord, let me be highly favored in Jesus' name.
29. Let men be without evil intent and favor me, let woman favor me, let both old and young favor me in Jesus' name.
30. Father Lord, let the good fruit of my labor flourish in Jesus' name.
31. Father Lord, destroy any accusing demon that tries to hinder me from receiving my blessings in Jesus' name.
32. Jesus, cause any strange hand dragging my blessings away from me to wither in the name of Jesus.
33. Lord Jesus, please remove every embargo in the way of Your will for my life in Jesus' name.
34. Lord, remove any stagnant positions, disappointments, hatred, and failures in the mighty name of Jesus Christ.
35. Any error of death against me, against my wife, against my children, against my siblings, against my friends, is destroyed in the mighty name of Jesus.
36. No weapon fashioned against me shall prosper, for I shall not die, but live to declare the glory of God.
37. Blood of Jesus, envelop my family and me in Jesus' name.
38. Any Goliath hindering my breakthroughs shall receive destruction in the mighty name of Jesus Christ. Lord, bind any hindering spirits so that I can hear Your words and hold them in my heart.
39. Oh Lord, it is written that we shall decree, and it shall be established, therefore as I decree in prayer establish it Lord, in Jesus' name.

40. Father Lord, let those who seek my downfall be gloried with shame, any hindering spirit that blocks favor from God, I destroy you in Jesus' name.

41. Oh Lord, You, said You would give Your angels charge over me to guide me lest I dash my foot against a stone. May Your angels guide me continually in Jesus' name.

42. Heavenly Father, save me from death, save me from sickness, all satanic war, witches' and wizards' war, and marine war, and let them be vanquished in Jesus' name.

43. Father Lord, rise up early with Your deadly weapon to fight for me.

44. Jehovah-Jireh, God who conquers all witches and wizards, conquer and destroy them, in Jesus' name.

45. Powers of household wickedness that obstruct my progress forward; make their efforts backfire by fire in Jesus' name.

46. I bind and paralyze every spirit from their destination in Jesus' name.

47. I destroy every spirit of backwardness that holds me back from purity in Jesus' name.

48. I reject every spirit of frustration and disappointment in Jesus' name.

49. I reject every spirit of setback and failure dedicated to me by household enemies; I crush their spirit in Jesus' name.

50. Where others have failed, I shall succeed and glory the name of the Lord in Jesus' name.

51. Lord Almighty arises and incubates me with wisdom, understanding, and knowledge in Jesus' name.

52. Heavenly Father, let every marital situation challenging my life bow to the power of God Almighty.

53. My faith and belief in my Lord Jesus arise and rebel against every spirit of demotion against my life in Jesus' name.

54. Heavenly Father, Everlasting Redeemer, I thank You for Your divine shield upon my life, my family, my siblings, and my friends in the matchless name of Jesus.

55. Father Lord, I thank You for answering my prayer today in Jesus' name.

56. Amen.

Chapter 3

Marriage Killers

Many Christian marriages are under the evil attacks, and the word of the Lord tells us:

For our struggle is not against flesh and blood, but against the rulers, against the powers, against the world forces of this darkness, against the spiritual forces of wickedness in the heavenly places. - Ephesians 6:12

Christians are in a spiritual battle with Satan and his demonic agents. He sees all of God's children as his enemy. His mission is to destroy us; one of his most vicious attacks is against Christian marriages.

> *The thief comes only to steal and kill and destroy; I came that they may have life, and have it abundantly. - John 10:10*

The enemy wants to destroy all believers, destroy their faith, and destroy their relationship with our Lord God. The strategy of the enemy is to destroy all Christian marriage and family relationships. We all need to be on the alert and guard our marriages and loved ones. Satan, attacking our marriages, does two things: First, he hurts our relationship with God; and second, he hurts our testimony to those who don't believe in God as well as our witness to those who do believe in Jesus, but may be spiritually immature.

If Satan has the power to destroy Christian marriages, then he can destroy Christ's testimony to unbelievers. Christians live by God's principles and yet their marriages are falling apart. This convinces the unbelievers to disbelieve any of God's principles because Satan has been controlling the believers' homes and is destroying their loved ones and their marriages.

God has a plan for marriage. As quoted above, John 10:10 gives us a warning and a promise. We should be alert and protect our loved ones and our marriages as the devil is on assignment to destroy all.

Build a marriage upon God's principles, and Satan and his demons have no power over it since God is the center of the marriage. Once the husband and wife are serious about God's principles and pray together, share issues together, and let God be God in their marriage, there is no way Satan can take charge, or take control of such a marriage because the God we serve is a faithful God and a provider. But if we lose track of God's principles, Satan would surely take charge of our marriages.

Satan is crafty, genius, and a master of deception. If he can get you, he will surely strive to make your loved ones feel disappointment and discouragement because of your behavior. You will feel frustration, anger, bitterness, and many other feelings that distract you from the love of God.

Many facing these attacks ask, "Why me, God?"

Satan is not omnipotent or omnipresent as God Almighty is, but Satan has assigned specialized legions, demons against Christians all over the world. These are spirits of marriage destruction. They initiate family strife, infidelity, marriage breaking, divorce, and general marital dysfunction or distress.

There is an evil spirit on assignment to destroy marriages going in home after home. Their main purpose is to destroy every good marriage. They usually begin their assignment by making sure lust and cheating take place in the marriage. They start by attacking the man and the woman by having uncontrollable sexual affairs, sex outside the marriage. These evil spirits lure men and women into watching pornographic movies that make them behave like animals, and start going after anything that moves outside of their marriages.

Pornographic sex is not real sex in the eyes of God. These are all evil acts and ungodly sexual acts — in a word, sin. As a result of this, marriages based on sex and self-gratification cannot last and will dissolve.

Many Christians are ignorant and even skeptical of the activities of the spirit of Jezebel. This spirit is well organized and prepared to destroy everyone that is ignorant with wicked tricks. We must fight the spirit of Jezebel—in the spirit and not in the flesh alone.

Some women and men go beyond that, if they can't find someone to fulfill their sexual desires when they need it, so they start attacking their poor dog that has been minding his own business to have sex with it. This is what we call household wickedness. This agent of darkness is one of the spirits of Jezebel's demons: Once they attack you, they will control your mind and your sexual urges. The spirits of household wickedness control all these forces.

There is so much sex that is not attributed to the marriage bed. Many people ignore the fact that God created sex for the pleasure of His people—man and woman, husband and wife only.

The husband must fulfill his duty to his wife, and likewise also the wife to her husband. The wife does not have authority over her own body, but the husband does; and likewise, also the husband does not have authority over his own body, but the wife does. – 1 Corinthians 7:3-4

There are some innocent families in which the spirit of household wickedness causes the spouse to misbehave in the marriage, and have extramarital affairs leading to divorce. How does this issue happen to innocent families or people? Some marriages receive a spell: Family members that are against their marriage can curse the marriage, envious friends can curse the marriage, some people can associate themselves in a wrong social gathering with devil worshippers, or some can live an ungodly lifestyle that invites these evil spirits into their life or home.

This world is evil. Some questions that Christians have asked:

Whom does the spirit of Jezebel possess? Who is attracted by Jezebel's spirit?

The more I try to avoid such temptation, the more evil tempts me. How do I control that?

21

Will I ever be able to avoid this uncomfortable desire and such a disgraceful lifestyle?

Can I be set free from the spirit of Jezebel's lifestyle since my sexual urges constantly rise above the roof?

One must seek deliverance in a healthy, balanced church or follow the simple instructions on how to be set free from such wicked spirits through aggressive prayers against the evil powers.

The Bible tells us about the spirit of Jezebel and her behavior!

I know your deeds, and your love and faith and service and perseverance, and that your deeds of late are greater than at first. But I have this against you, that you tolerate the woman Jezebel, who calls herself a prophetess, and she teaches and leads My bondservants astray so that they commit acts of immorality and eat things sacrificed to idols. I gave her time to repent, and she does not want to repent of her immorality. Behold, I will throw her on a bed of sickness, and those who commit adultery with her into great tribulation, unless they repent of her deeds. And I will kill her children with pestilence, and all the churches will know that I am He who searches the minds and hearts; and I will give to each one of you according to your deeds. But I say to you, the rest who are in Thyatira, who do not hold this teaching, who have not known the deep things Satan, as they call them — I place no other burden on you. Nevertheless, what you have, hold fast until I come.

- Revelation 2:19-25

Who is this spirit of Jezebel? She is one of the powerful agents of darkness, queen of the coast, and numerous demons work together with her.

Some of the demons she works with are spirit of failure, spirit of disgrace, spirit of embarrassment, spirit of shame, spirit of gender manipulation, spirit of prostitution, spirit of bestiality, spirits of transgender, spirit of womanizer, spirit of drug abuse, spirit of alcoholism, spirit of gambling, spirit of confusion, spirit of household wickedness, and spirits of Incubus and Succubus. These spirits always travel together with one agenda: to destroy happy homes, marriages, families, and loved ones. These spirits specialize in attacking many powerful men and women of God.

Our Lord Jesus Christ calls this spirit of Jezebel a false teacher that leads His servants astray. Jezebel was a very powerful wicked queen, and she was the wife of a passive king called Ahab. She was a false prophetess who worshiped the false god, Baal. Baal was the demon god of prosperity, god of fertility and sex. Child sacrifices were common. Commander Jehu commanded several eunuchs to kill her. Prophecy was fulfilled when the dogs ate her remains. Jezebel was a witch, and her spirit of witchcraft is still in operation in churches today.

Spirit of Jezebel is sociopathic with her associate demons. They gain power by destroying others. They manage to get in position of authority, and are difficult to displace once in power. Characteristics of the Jezebel spirit are:

- They are controlling, manipulative and bossy.
- They are very intimidating, threatening others with their power or position of authority. They bully anyone they can.
- They never admit they are wrong.
- They recruit others in their charge against their victims.
- They are not sympathetic to their victims.
- They always claim religious sentiments.

This spirit attacks both men and women. Jezebel encourages believers to worship idols and commit sexual sin. This spirit encourages ministers to have sexual affairs with their congregation members. This spirit encourages many men and women in power to fail by committing sexual sins. This spirit likes to mingle with the people of God, especially in churches, causing all kind of confusion and abominations. Jezebel specializes in ensnaring and convincing people to follow her teachings that will lead them to rebellion against God Almighty. Many people fall for her charm and give in to idol worship in their lives, the same as King Ahab did when he married Jezebel.

The Bible tells us:

It came about, as though it had been a trivial thing for him to walk in the sins of Jeroboam the son of Nebat, that he married Jezebel the daughter of Ethbaal king of the Sidonians, and went to serve Baal and worshiped him. - 1 Kings 16:31

Spirit of Jezebel's goal is to kill the true prophets of God. Prophet Elijah, after challenging and killing more than four hundred of Queen Jezebel's false Baal prophets, ran out into the desert in a panic after receiving a letter from Queen Jezebel swearing that she would kill him. Prophet Elijah became so intimidated that he ran for his life.

Once again, Jezebel's predictions were false as her prophecies usually are, and Prophet Elijah did not die.

The power of God is above all evil, and Jezebel's curse was void and null.

Jezebel is good with seduction, deception, and manipulation through controlling your mind and your destiny. Jezebel is the woman who controls and runs the home. She is in charge; one cannot speak when she is speaking. She is a very dominating woman.

Jezebel usually mixes religious terms in her speech to appear godly, but her lifestyle doesn't reflect godliness. Following her lifestyle will lead you into rebellion, anger, bitterness, resentment, disappointment, failure, disgrace, strife, and total darkness. She has no compassion for those who offend her. She keeps track of all offenses, and uses them to her advantage. The Jezebel spirit specializes in causing confusion and rejoices in causing strife. She is full of lies, deceit, and disappointments.

The Bible tells us:

When Jezebel heard that Naboth had been stoned and was dead, Jezebel said to Ahab, Arise, take possession of the vineyard of Naboth, the Jezreelite, which he refused to give you for money; for Naboth is not alive, but dead. When Ahab heard that Naboth was dead, Ahab arose to go down to the vineyard of Naboth the Jezreelite, to take possession of it.

- 1 Kings 21:15-16

King Ahab's negligence in curtailing Queen Jezebel's wicked behaviors made him an impersonator of Jezebel. Ahab was an evil man, possessing the same spirit as his wife Jezebel, as he mocked the prophet Elijah and called him intimidating names.

When Ahab saw Elijah, Ahab said to him, is this you, you troublers of Israel? 1 Kings 18:17

The word of the Lord says marriage is a union between man and woman.

For this reason, a man shall leave his father and his mother, and be joined to his wife; and they shall become one flesh.

– Genesis 2:24

For this reason, a man shall leave his father and mother and the two shall become one flesh; so they are no longer two, but one flesh. What therefore God has joined together, let no man separate.

- Mark 10:7-9

For we also once were foolish ourselves, disobedient, deceived, enslaved to various lusts and pleasures, spending our life in malice and envy, hateful, hating one another. But when the kindness of God our Savior and His love for mankind appeared, He saved us, not on the basis of deeds which we have done in righteousness, but according to His mercy, by the washing of regenerating and renewing by the Holy Spirit. Blessed be the God and Father of our Lord Jesus Christ, who has redeemed us from the kingdom of darkness, and has blessed us with every spiritual blessing in the heavenly places in Christ Jesus. – Titus 3:3-5

And I will bless those who bless you, and the one who curses you I will curse. And in you all the families of the earth will be blessed. – Genesis 12:3 3

The wise woman builds her house, but the foolish tears it down with her own hands. – Proverbs 14:1

Yet you say, "For what reason?" Because the Lord has been a witness between you and the wife of your youth, against whom you have dealt treacherously, though she is your companion and your wife by covenant. But not one has done so who has a remnant of the Spirit. And what did that one do while he was seeking a godly offspring? Take heed then to your spirit, and let no one deal treacherously against the wife of your youth. For I hate divorce, says the Lord, the God of Israel, and him who covers his garment with wrong, says the Lord of hosts. So, take heed to your spirit that you do not deal treacherously.

– Malachi 2:14-16

The devil started his attack from the Garden of Eden. He has converted many homes into a satanic playground. I pray that the God of Isaac, God of Jacob, and God of Abraham will take charge, take total control of every situation you're in, and stir up righteous indignation within you to attack your attackers through this prayer program.

Has Satan got a grip on your marriage?

- Here are some excellent questions to see if he does:
- Are you experiencing turbulence in your marriage?
- Are you experiencing nightmares in your marriage?
- Do you feel like there is a mountain crushing your marriage?
- Is there a power of the darkness tampering with your sex life?
- Is there a spirit of Incubus and Succubus misusing your sex organs?
- Is there a spirit of Gender Manipulation confusing who you are?
- Is a spirit husband or a spirit wife blocking you from getting on with your life?
- Is the place you once called home under a satanic attack?
- Is Satan using your home as a satanic playground?

If you answered yes to any of the above questions, then this book is for you. I invite you to build a problem burial ground.

I pray that the God of Elijah shall certainly use this program to turn every uncontrollable situation in your marriage into peace, love, joy, sound mind, and harmony in Jesus' name.

An excellent wife, who can find? For her worth is far above jewels. The heart of her husband trusts in her, and he will have no lack of gain. She does him good and not evil all the days of her life.

– Proverbs 31:10-12 10

So that at the name of Jesus **every knee will bow**, of those who are in Heaven and on Earth and under the earth. – Philippians 2:10

Prayer

1. Father Lord, I am a sinner; I ask for forgiveness, forgive all my sins in Jesus' name.
2. God Almighty, take charge, take control over every department in my marriage in Jesus' name.
3. Any agents of darkness bargaining for my marriage, Heavenly Father, destroy them without recognition in Jesus' name.
4. Any powers of the night using my finances to cause problems in my marriage, Father God, destroy them by fire in Jesus' name.
5. Evil powers militating against the divine purpose of my marriage, in Jesus' name, I command you to collide with the Rock of Ages.
6. Lord, paralyze evil powers preventing my marriage in Jesus' name.
7. Jehovah Lord, destroy all evil giants standing against peace and unity in my marriage with Your thunder fire in Jesus' name.
8. Any spirit of household wickedness calling evil rise against my family expire now in Jesus' name.
9. Marital unfaithfulness troubling my marriage the word of the Lord casts you out in Jesus' name.

10. Gadget of marital destruction upon my marriage, crumble now in Jesus' name.

11. Lord Jesus, make Your axe of fire cut every root of my marital problems into pieces in Jesus' name.

12. Heavenly Father, send confusion to the camp of my oppressors over my marriage in Jesus' name.

13. Everlasting Redeemer, redeem my marriage from the hands of the wicked in Jesus' name.

14. Jehovah Lord, abort every satanic pregnancy in my marriage and in the life of both my spouse and me right now in Jesus' name.

15. I nullify evil desires, plans of divorce, and separation against my marriage in Jesus' name.

16. Jehovah-Jireh, confuse the source of the problems over marriage in Jesus' name.

17. Jezebel spirit, hear me and hear me well: You have no place to wreck and destroy my home in Jesus' name.

18. God that answers by fire, destroy every spirit of misunderstanding between my husband/wife and me in Jesus' name.

19. Fountain of discomfort over my marriage, dry up now in Jesus' name.

20. Every mountain over my marriage, crumble in Jesus' name.

21. Evil arrow fired by legions into my marriage, burn to ashes in Jesus' name.

22. Most High God, make every power of the oppressors against my marriage rise up against each other in Jesus' name.

23. , Lord Jesus, consume the evil powers bragging against my God with Your thunder fire in Jesus' name.

24. I refuse to listen to the voice of Satan over my marriage in Jesus' name.

25. Lord Jesus, let the word of the Lord pierce through the heart of my oppressors, in Jesus' name.

26. Silence evil storms over my marriage now in Jesus' name.

27. Father Lord, turn everything dead in any department of my marriage into goodness and life in Jesus' name.
28. I bind and paralyze all evil marriage destroyers and anti-marriage forces in the matchless name of Jesus Christ.
29. Blood of Jesus, pursue every negative force over my marriage in Jesus' name.
30. Thunder fires of God destroy all demons attached to my marriage in Jesus' name.
31. Every stubborn demon bargaining for my marriage, collide with the Rock of Ages in Jesus' name.
32. Jehovah, Yahweh, I thank You for delivering my marriage from the hands of the household wickedness in Jesus' name.
33. Whenever my family name is mentioned for evil, fire of God, attach my family name with fire and consume the evil spirits with holy fire in Jesus' name.
34. I bind and paralyze all marriage destroyers against my marriage in Jesus' name.
35. Fires of the Holy Ghost destroy evil manipulators over my marriage in Jesus' name.
36. Every hidden anti-marriage force fighting against my marriage be thou destroyed in Jesus' name.
37. I break every evil vow and covenant over my marriage in Jesus' name.
38. Blood of Jesus wash away all filthy issues in my marriage in Jesus' name.
39. Powers of the night fueling marriage conflicts and hostilities in my life bow to the power of God Almighty in Jesus' name.
40. I decree and declare fire of God to rip my marriage from the hands of the destroyers in Jesus' name.
41. I bind all powers eating up the love in my marriage in Jesus' name.
42. I bind and paralyze every spirit of Jezebel attacking my home in Jesus' name.
43. Lord Jesus, correct every mistake and error I have made in my marriage in Jesus' name.

44. I break the chain of every evil journey of destruction upon my marriage in Jesus' name.
45. Marital problems with unknown causes affecting my life, bow to the power of God Almighty now in Jesus' name.
46. Uproot every evil tree planted against my marriage, now in Jesus' name.
47. I arrest the arresters of my marriage in Jesus' name.
48. I withdraw my marriage from the hands of the wicked in Jesus' name.
49. Whenever evil spirits do not want to see my marriage prosper, Father Lord, manifest mightily over my marriage in Jesus' name.
50. God of Elijah, send down Your holy fire over my marriage in Jesus' name.
51. Father Lord, give me extra love for my spouse in Jesus' name.
52. Jesus of Nazareth, please help me with the power and fire of Your love over my marriage in Jesus' name.
53. I shall love my spouse whether my enemies like it or not in Jesus' name.
54. I shall see the beauty of my spouse whether our enemies like it or not in Jesus' name.
55. I shall kiss my spouse with love and compassion whether our enemies like it or not in Jesus' name.
56. Father Lord, pour extra currents of love over my marriage in Jesus' name.
57. Father Lord, give me extra affection for my spouse in Jesus' name.
58. Evil eyes monitoring my marriage be blindfolded and lose track of my marriage now in Jesus' name.
59. I break my marriage loose from any demonic altar in Jesus' name.
60. Evil chains tying down my marriage shatter to pieces in Jesus' name.
61. I break the backbone of evil stagnancy over my marriage in Jesus' name.

62. I break the backbone of any spirit whose assignment is to hinder my spouse and me from full deliverance from any marriage killer in Jesus' name.
63. I break the backbone of the spirit of confusion within my marriage in Jesus' name.
64. I break the backbone of the spirit of disgrace within my marriage in Jesus' name.
65. I break the backbone of the spirit of evil tongue and evil words within my marriage in Jesus' name.
66. I shall enjoy the fruitfulness of my marriage whether my enemies like it or not in Jesus' name.
67. I proclaim total favor and breakthroughs within my marriage in Jesus' name.
68. Troubles in my marriage dissolve as solutions prevail in Jesus' name.
69. Jehovah Lord, anoint me with favor and restoration within my marriage in Jesus' name.
70. Everlasting Redeemer, I thank You for deliverance for my marriage in Jesus' name.
71. Amen.

You must command the evil spirits to leave you.

You must continue to rebuke them *seven times* by the power of the blood of Jesus Christ, and they will leave you in Jesus' name.

Say out loud: You evil spirits that cause me to be bound to the attacks of marriage killers, I renounce you and all your associate demons, and all your works in my life; I command you in the mighty name of Jesus Christ to lose your grip and release me and my marriage now; by the thunder fire of God, in the matchless name of Jesus Christ I pray. Amen.

Chapter 4

Abuse in Marriage

Abusive marriages usually begin when a couple tries to resolve a conflict the wrong way. One side may make an effort for resolution, but the other side may resist the proposal increasing force until the spouse browbeats the other into submission. There are healthy ways to disagree. However, every fight in the marriage is an example of abuse because it uses the tactic of emotional or physical force to resolve a conflict instead of respecting each other.

Abusive Husband

- Why does a man beat his wife as if she were a punching bag?
- What exactly went wrong in their love when they met for the first time?
- Is it okay for a husband to beat his spouse?
- Is it a sin for a husband to abuse his wife?
- Many men get angry over stupid things and beat their wives.

A man beating his wife is taboo, a complete curse. A wife is a helper to her husband. Once a man starts raising his hand against his helper, many good things begin to fade out spiritually as well as physically in their lives. There are many powerful men in positions of authority—ministers and leaders in organizations—who handle conflicts with force. Suddenly, many good things start going sour in their lives. Internal issues at home start spiraling out of control: Their stories stay behind closed doors, such as beating their wives, emotional and verbal abuse against their wives, and harassment against their wives. This behavior curses them to become nothing in life.

Regardless of what goes wrong, no one is perfect. A man is a leader at home, and a leader must always set an example in his kingdom. A leader without blessings from God is a leader without a kingdom. A leader must fear God, and a leader must obey the principles of God. He must pray with his family, together in one accord, and on a daily basis.

God has blessed men to be leaders in their family, but once men start misusing the power God has ordained them as the husband, Satan starts taking over his life and starts turning it upside down, which deeply affects the family. Once men allow Satan into their family, Satan's assignment is to kill and destroy and suppress the family into destruction, divorce, or separation.

There are many married men that beat and mistreat their wives. They are under satanic oppression. When they finish beating their wives, they become sorry and start apologizing to their wives, and promise not to do it again. Master Satan controls the majority of these men.

Satan has many men today in his kingdom, using them as he pleases. If things don't go their way, Satan uses the power of anger, bitterness, and resentment, so they abuse and misuse everything around them including their wives and children.

If you are in a relationship and experiencing such behavior in your marriage, increase your prayer life, and seek deliverance because your marriage is under a satanic attack.

For our struggle is not against flesh and blood, but against the rulers, against the powers, against the world forces of this darkness, against the spiritual forces of wickedness in the heavenly places. – Ephesians 6:12

It is a sin for a husband to beat his wife, and it hinders the couple's prayer lives.

You husbands in the same way, live with your wives in an understanding way, as with someone weaker, since she is a woman;

and show her honor as a fellow heir of the grace of life, so that your prayers will not be hindered. – 1 Peter 3:7

But not one has done so who has a remnant of the Spirit. And what did that one do while he was seeking a godly offspring? Take heed then to your spirit, and let no one deal treacherously against the wife of your youth. – Malachi 2:15

Husbands, love your wives and do not be embittered against them. –Colossians 3:19

A man's discretion makes him slow to anger, and it is his glory to overlook a transgression. – Proverbs 19:11

Abusive Wife

- Why it that many women are so abusive to their husbands?
- What exactly went wrong in their love when they met for the first time?
- Is it right for a woman to be verbally abusive against her husband?
- Is it okay for a woman to deny her husband from intimacy?
- Is it a sin for a woman to abuse her husband?

Many women get angry over stupid things then deny their husband sex or other things that would serve as a punishment. Satan has many women enslaved with one or more spirits of Jezebel to wreak havoc over marriages. A wife oppressed by this evil spirit can exhibit an ungodly interest in material wealth and instant gratification. She is overbearing, controlling, and demanding. She can be consumed by distrust, jealousy, and possessiveness. She may be focused on outward appearances and self-promoting ambitions. She will try to force her husband into spiritual submission to control him, and this overturns God's order for marriage.

But I want you to realize that the head of every man is Christ, and the head of the woman is man and the head of Christ is God. - 1. Corinthians 11:3

Wives can be just as abusive as men with verbal attacks, and at times, physical, attacks. It usually starts with disagreements that escalate out of control. Women will sometimes react in kind to verbal abuse so that the home becomes a place of razor-sharp, hurtful words. Abusive wives tend to get violent by throwing things at their husbands rather than punching or hitting. However, slapping and hitting is abuse, and some wives resort to physical abuse. This is ungodly behavior, and a sin. Many Christian women lose self-control, and exhibit this behavior.

How should I respond to a physically abusive wife?

Is it okay for a man to leave an abusive wife and look for a better wife? No, it is not okay for a man to leave their abusive wife. Divorce is not an answer! Marriage vows are for worse or better.

"For I hate divorce," says the Lord, the God of Israel, "and him who covers his garment with wrong", says the Lord of hosts. "So take heed to your spirit that you do not deal treacherously." – Malachi 2:16

If your wife is an abusive woman, it is your responsibility as a man to help her in prayer and lead her in biblical counseling. There is no situation that prayer cannot answer!

Sometimes the issues you are going through in your marriage could be spiritual issues, as many times there are spirit husbands and spirit wives that cause many conflicts in marriages, or it could be a spirit of depression, spirit of bitterness, or spirit of anger that has been troubling your wife to the point she needs deliverance.

How is your prayer life at home?

Do you spend quality time reading the Bible and praying together with your family at home?

Or do you just pray alone?

A husband is the leader at home; therefore, it is the responsibility of the husband to make sure every night and every morning he gathers the family together and reads the word of the Lord and prays with the family!

But you don't know how to pray? You can always start with Genesis 1:1 to Revelations 22:21 reading a chapter or a verse a day, and pray a simple prayer such as:

1. Jehovah Lord, I thank You for the breath You have given me.
2. Father Lord, I thank You for the beautiful family You have given me.
3. Heavenly Father, I ask for Your divine protection upon my family.
4. Lord Jesus, cover my family with the blood of Jesus Christ.
5. God Almighty, shield and protect my family and me from the hands of the wicked in Jesus' name.
6. Everlasting Father, I thank You for answer, my prayer in Jesus' name.
7. Amen.

Is your marriage Christ-centered?

Most of the marriages today are not Christ-centered marriages; therefore, Satan has dripped evil over them causing all sorts of problems in so many marriages today.

You can turn around the issues in your marriage by calling out to Jesus Christ to rescue your marriage. As you pray these prayers in faith, our heavenly Father, Jehovah Lord God Almighty, will pour out His divine favor over your marriage, and cleanse the evil from it. He will transform the abuse in your marriage into a Godly divine favor and perfection.

> Marriage is to be held in honor among all, and the bed is to be undefiled; for fornicators and adulterers God will judge.
>
> – Hebrews 13:4
>
> So they are no longer two, but one flesh. What therefore God has joined together, let no man separate.
>
> – Matthew 19:6
>
> Finally, be strong in the Lord and in the strength of His might. Put on the full armor of God, so that you will be able to stand

firm against the schemes of the devil. For our struggle is not against flesh and blood, but against the rulers, against the powers, against the world forces of this darkness, against the spiritual forces of wickedness in the heavenly places. Therefore, take up the full armor of God, so that you will be able to resist in the evil day, and having done everything, to stand firm.

– Ephesians 6:10-13

God Almighty has given us power above all evil; call in His name, and Jehovah will destroy every evil throne sitting in your marriage.

Prayer for Both Husband and Wife

Everlasting Father, I ask for forgiveness, Father Lord, for any sin in my life that would hinder my prayer from being answered. Heavenly Father, forgive me. Anyone I have sinned against that I do not know about, Lord Jesus, forgive me in Jesus' name.

I loose, myself from the bondage of satanic controlling that is causing the abuse in my marriage in Jesus' name. I shield my marriage with the blood of Jesus Christ. I soak my spouse in the blood of Jesus Christ. I soak my family in the blood of Jesus Christ.

I have sinned against my spouse and against you, Lord Jesus. Heavenly Father, I have done many ugly and filthy things against my spouse. The Alpha and Omega forgive me, and deliver me from the hands of the oppressors. I know deep inside me the devil has been using me through spirits of anger, bitterness, drugs, alcohol, and fornication. Lord Jesus help me; set me free because I am tired of Satan controlling my life and my marriage. The Lord God Almighty, I know You died on the cross of Calvary for my sins. I accept You as my personal savor and Lord. Heavenly Father, touch my life and destroy any filthy garment Satan has prepared for me.

Lord Jesus, break me, mold me, and use me as You please, deliver me from the hands of the wicked. Father Lord, take absolute control in every department in my life and heal me where I need healing, transform me where I need transformation, and deliver me where I need deliverance in Jesus' precious name. Amen.

1. I bind and paralyze every hostility and conflict between my spouse and me in Jesus' name.
2. I take back my marriage from the hands of the marriage abusers in Jesus' name.
3. I take back my marriage from the hands of the marriage manipulators in Jesus' name.
4. Fire of God burn to ashes every power of marriage destroyers sitting on the throne of my marriage in Jesus' name.
5. Household wickedness holding onto my marriage release it now in Jesus' name.
6. Father Lord, deliver my marriage from the hands of the marriage destroyers in Jesus' name.
7. Evil powers toying with the mind of my spouse making things miserable in my marriage collide with the Rock of Ages.
8. I set my marriage free from the hands of abusers and home wreckers in Jesus' name.
9. I challenge the home wreckers by the power of God Almighty.
10. External forces interfering in my marriage be completely paralyzed in Jesus.
11. Power of the night on assignment to wreck my marriage through abusive conditions, be gone. My spouse is set free by the power of the blood of Jesus Christ.
12. I destroy every evil power eating away the love of my spouse to stay married in Jesus' name.
13. Strangers of the night on assignment to destroy my marriage my marriage is not your candidate in Jesus' name.
14. Blood of Jesus, Holy Ghost fire, pursue and overwhelm all strangers of the night bargaining for my marriage, toss them into the lake of fire in Jesus' name.

15. Issues in my marriage impossible to solve, fire of God take charge and take control of the situation in Jesus' name.

16. Holy Ghost, convict and deliver my spouse from the hands of evil seducers in Jesus' name.

17. Heavenly Father, I come into Your presence; I ask that You remove all evil strangers in my life in Jesus' name.

18. -Everlasting Redeemer, any assigned demons controlling my life, scatter them with Your thunder fire in Jesus' name.

19. Whenever my family name is mentioned for evil, Jehovah Lord let my family name be attached with fire and consume the evil ones with Your thunder fire in Jesus' name.

20. Any evil gathering concerning my marriage, Father Lord, scatter them in Jesus' name.

21. Evil curses concerning my life through rage, bitterness, anger, and frustration over my life, Father Lord, turn all curses into blessings in Jesus' name.

22. I receive deliverance from every evil plantation designed to bring my marriage under the bondage of the devil in Jesus' name.

23. I receive deliverance from every evil plantation designed to bring hostility between my spouse and me under the bondage of the devil in Jesus' name.

24. I receive deliverance from every evil plantation designed to bring anger and bitterness between my spouse and me under the bondage of the devil in Jesus' name.

25. I deliver my marriage from the hands of the home wreckers in Jesus' name.

26. Any power toying with my mind, trying to destroy my marriage, Father Lord, cut them off in Jesus' name.

27. Power of the night bargaining for my marriage, Father Lord, cut them off in Jesus' name.

28. Satan, hear me and hear me well, you cannot break my marriage through anger, bitterness, and yelling at my husband in Jesus' name.

29. I command failure, frustration, and disappointment to come upon the evil strangers in my marriage in Jesus' name.

30. You, Spirit of Disappointment and Failures shouting at my marriage catch the fire of God in Jesus' name.

31. Jehovah Lord, deliver me from the spirit of oppression on assignment upon my life in Jesus' name.

32. Jehovah Lord, deliver my marriage from evil spirits on assignment of oppression upon my marriage in Jesus' name.

33. Every evil gathering concerning my marriage, Father Lord, let Your thunder fire scatter them in Jesus' name.

34. Evil curse concerning my life through rage, bitterness, anger, and frustration over my marriage, Father Lord turns all curses upon my marriage into blessings in Jesus' name.

35. Heavenly Father, deliver my marriage from every rage that the evils have planted against it in Jesus' name.

36. I receive deliverance from every evil plantation designed to bring hostility between my spouse and me under the bondage of the devil in Jesus' name.

37. I receive deliverance from every evil plantation designed to bring anger and bitterness between my spouse and me under the bondage of the devil in Jesus' name.

38. Heavenly Father, deliver my marriage from the hands of the powers of the night and all associate demons in Jesus' name.

39. Any power playing games with my mind trying to destroy my marriage, Father Lord, cut them off in Jesus' name.

40. Assigned demons bargaining for my marriage, Father Lord, destroy them in Jesus' name.

41. Satan, hear me and hear me well, you cannot break my marriage through anger, bitterness and beating of my wife; your assignment is over in Jesus' name.

42. Blood of Jesus chase evil strangers in my life into the lake of fire in Jesus' name.

43. Every stronghold of household witchcraft attacking my marriage, perish now in Jesus' name.

44. Spirits of household wickedness that are after my marriage collide with the Rock of Ages in Jesus' name.

45. Evil deposits against my marriage perish now in Jesus' name.

46. Lord Jesus, break every yoke of backsliding against my marriage in Jesus' name.

47. Evil powers enchanting against my life perish in Jesus' name.

48. Evil powers enchanting against my marriage perish in Jesus' name.

49. Powers of the night on assignment against my marriage lose your hold in Jesus' name.

50. I disentangle my spouse and myself from every witchcraft cage in Jesus' name.

51. I disentangle my marriage from every witchcraft cage in the mighty name of Jesus Christ.

52. Every hidden evil arrow of wickedness over my marriage backfires by fire in Jesus' name.

53. Heavenly Father, break every yoke of iniquity upon my marriage in Jesus' name.

54. Spirit of abuser challenging my marriage life, catch the fire of God in Jesus' name.

55. Heavenly Father, scatter every evil gathering upon my marriage in Jesus' name.

56. Heavenly Father, turn all curses upon my marriage into blessings in Jesus' name.

57. Jehovah Lord, I thank You for delivering my marriage from the hands of the wicked in Jesus' name.

58. Blood of Jesus pursue and overwhelm every agent of darkness on assignment to destroy my marriage side by side into the lake of fire in Jesus' name.

59. Everlasting Redeemer, I thank You for delivering my life from the hands of Satan and his agents in Jesus' name.

60. Lord Jesus, I come into Your presence, I ask that any evil strangers in my life be destroyed; Heavenly Father let Your thunder fire destroy them completely out of my life in Jesus' name.

61. Father Lord, the same fire Prophet Elijah has commanded to destroy the evil prophets of Baal, let that fire destroy all agents of darkness controlling my life, my family, my marriage, and my home in Jesus' name.

62. I take authority over any powers, any assigned agent of darkness controlling my life, raising anger, bitterness, and oppressions into my life, against my marriage in Jesus' name.

63. Any evil gathering concerning my marriage father Lord scatter them in Jesus' name.

64. Evil curses concerning my life through rage, bitterness, anger and frustration over my life Father Lord, turn all curses into blessings in Jesus' name.

65. I receive deliverance from every evil plantation designed to bring my marriage under the bondage of the devil in Jesus' name.

66. I receive deliverance from every evil plantation designed to bring hostility between my spouse and me under the bondage of the devil in Jesus' name.

67. I receive deliverance from every evil plantation of the spirit of rejection, spirit of rebellion, spirit of bitterness, spirit of unforgiveness, spirit of depression and spirit of murder from my ancestors against my life and family in Jesus' name.

68. I receive deliverance from the bondage of the devil, and from every evil plantation designed to bring anger and bitterness between my spouse and me in Jesus' name.

69. I deliver my marriage from the hands of the home wreckers in Jesus' name.

70. I destroy every sea demon challenging my marriage in Jesus' name.

71. I put on the armor of God against any spirits of destruction, trying to destroy my life and my family in Jesus' name.

72. Father Lord, cut off all powers of the night bargaining for my marriage, in Jesus' name.

73. Satan, hear me and hear me well, you cannot break my marriage; I dedicate my marriage to Christ Jesus.

74. I command failure, frustration, and disappointment to come upon the evil strangers in my marriage in Jesus' name.

75. By the authority of Jesus, all spirits of abuse that are controlling my life I send to the pit, in Jesus' name.

76. You, spirits of abuse, playing tricks in my spouse's mind, catch the fire of God.

77. Father Lord, deliver me from spirits of oppression on assignment upon my life in Jesus' name.

78. Blood of Jesus, wash away every filthy garment draped over my marriage in Jesus' name.

79. Blood of Jesus pursue and overwhelm agents of darkness on assignment to destroy my marriage, escort them into the lake of fire in Jesus' name.

80. Heavenly Father, I thank You for delivering my life from the hands of Satan and his agents in Jesus' name.

81. Every agent of darkness toying with the mind of my spouse, hear the Word of the Lord.

82. Angels of war, make frustration and disappointment come upon and destroy the spirits of abusive marriage attacking my marriage in Jesus' name.

83. Powers of abusive marriage fueling problems into my marriage die in Jesus' name.

84. Everlasting Father, let the angels of the living God pursue the spirit behind abusive marriage from my home in Jesus.

85. Armor of God, destroy every spirit of abusive marriage destroying my marriage in Jesus.

86. Favor of God, overwhelm every area of my life, and bring my spouse back into normal marriage stage in Jesus' name.

87. I refuse to allow Satan and the spirits of abusive spouse to take over my marriage in Jesus' name.
88. Agent of darkness on assignment against my home, my home is not your candidate; collide with the Rock of Ages.
89. I break the power of every spirit of abusive marriage fashioned against my marriage in Jesus' name.
90. I bind and paralyze every spirit of failure working in my home against my marriage in Jesus' name.
91. Fire of God, set my spouse free from every evil attack of bondage in Jesus' name.
92. Jezebel spirits controlling the organs of my spouse die in Jesus' name.
93. Jezebel spirit, playing games with the mind of my spouse bow to the power of God Almighty.
94. Father Lord, cause the spirits of Jezebel to release my spouse from every form of bondage in Jesus' name.
95. Agents of marital unfaithfulness, release my spouse from all evil marital bondage in Jesus' name.
96. Father Lord, by the power of the blood of Jesus Christ, pursue all spirits of abusive marriage attacking my home and marriage until they collide with the Rock of Ages.
97. I release my spouse free from all satanic bondage in Jesus' name.
98. Spirit of flirtation, spirit of Delilah, Spirit of unholy thoughts playing tricks in my spouse's mind die in Jesus' name.
99. I break every curse over my spouse by the power of the blood of Jesus Christ.
100. Heavenly Father, break every evil vow over my marriage in Jesus' name.
101. Heavenly Father, break every evil covenant over my marriage in Jesus' name.
102. I break every dark resistance challenging my marriage in Jesus' name.

103. I break every evil authority over my marriage in Jesus' name.
104. Holy Ghost fire breaks the backbone of marriage destroyers in Jesus' name.
105. Any powers of abusive marriage interfering with my marriage die in Jesus' name.
106. I bind and cast out bondage of marriage killers against my marriage in Jesus' name.
107. Every stronghold of household witchcraft attacking my marriage perishes now in Jesus' name.
108. Spirits of household wickedness after my marriage collide with the Rock of Ages in Jesus' name.
109. Evil deposits against my marriage perish now in Jesus' name.
110. Lord Jesus breaks every yoke of backwardness against my marriage in Jesus' name.
111. Every power enchanting against my life perishes in Jesus' name.
112. Powers of the night on assignment against my marriage lose your hold in Jesus'
113. Heavenly Father, break every yoke of iniquity upon my marriage in Jesus' name.
114. Spirit of abuse challenging my married life catch the fire of God in Jesus' name.
115. Heavenly Father, scatter every evil gathering upon my marriage in Jesus' name.
116. Heavenly Father, turn all curses upon my marriage into blessings in Jesus' name.
117. Jehovah Lord, I thank You for delivering my marriage from the hands of the wicked in Jesus' name.
118. Amen.

You must command the evil spirits to leave you.

You must continue to rebuke them *seven times* by the power of the blood of Jesus Christ, and they will leave you in Jesus' name.

You evil spirits that cause me to be bound to the attacks of marriage killers, I renounce you and all your associate demons, and all your works in my life; I command you in the mighty name of Jesus Christ to lose your grip and release me and my marriage now; by the thunder fire of God, in the matchless name of Jesus Christ I pray. Amen.

Chapter 5

Destroying Spirit of Pornography

So many people have questions about pornography, and questions about how this activity affects marriages. Their questions are very similar to these.

Why is it that many people are addicted to pornography?

Is it true that many homes are breaking up due to the issues of pornography?

Can pornography really destroy my marriage?

I have heard stories like the ones below as well.

I started watching pornography at age eight; I watch it every little chance I get. I've tried to stop many times but the more I try, the more I felt a voice inside me drawing me closer to it. I believe I'm hooked on pornography because I've been watching it for many years, and I am now 72 years old. How can I stop this secret habit of mine?

~oOo~

I started looking at porn magazines from high school when some of my schoolmates brought them; ever since, I've been hooked on it. There is not a single night I don't watch porn videos on the Internet; how can I stop getting my eyes massaged from the power of pornography?

~oOo~

My boyfriend introduced me to pornography videos while I was in college. We are no longer together and I am a happily married woman, but secretly I still watch pornography, and I believe that it is now destroying my marriage. I love it so much. But how can I stop watching them?

~oOo~

I am from a strong Christian home, both of my parents are strong believers, and I've been well trained in Christianity ever since I was six years old, but somehow, I've become addicted to pornography. I used to look at the porn magazines then go to the bathroom and masturbate. I am now a grown man married with three children, but I am still struggling with pornography. How can I be set free?

~oOo~

If pornography is sin, then why did God create it?

Is it true that there is a spirit that controls the habit of pornography?

Yes, pornography is a sin. God did not create sin. It was a man's choice to disobey God in the Garden of Eden. Since then, humankind has been plagued with the sinful nature. We live in a fallen world, and sin is part of that fallen world. Apostle John described the sin as the lust of the flesh. The lust of the eye has led many into this sinful act. Pornography, in general, is lusting after the flesh with your eye.

Pornography has destroyed many lives. Pornography has led many into masturbation addiction, and has destroyed many marriages because husbands and wives, after watching the pornography, expect their spouse to perform the same as the pornography they watched. In turn, this leads to broken marriages.

Let's hear what the Bible says about pornography.

> *For all that is in the world, the lust of the flesh and the lust of the eyes and the boastful pride of life, is not from the Father, but is from the world. – 1 John 2:16*

> *Do not desire her beauty in your heart, nor let her capture you with her eyelids. For on account of a harlot one is reduced to a loaf of bread, and an adulteress hunts for the precious life. Can a man take fire in his bosom and his clothes not be burned? Or can a man walk on hot coals and his feet not be scorched?*

> – Proverbs 6:25-28

> *But I say to you that everyone who looks at a woman with lust for her has already committed adultery with her in his heart.*

> – Matthew 5:28

God created sex to be between one man and one woman. All sex outside marriage is a sin. Exploiting sex is a sin. Sex inside the marriage is not sin because God, our creator, created it. Exploiting pornography is a sin because man, in his greediness, invented it.

Being darkened in their understanding, excluded from the life of God because of the ignorance that is in them, because of the hardness of their heart and they, having become callous, have given themselves over to sensuality for the practice of every kind of impurity with greediness. –Ephesians 4:18-19

Now flee from youthful lusts and pursue righteousness, faith, love, and peace, with those who call on the Lord from a pure heart. – 2 Timothy 2:22

Flee immorality. Every other sin that a man commits is outside the body, but the immoral man sins against his own body. Or do you not know that your body is a temple of the Holy Spirit who is in you, whom you have from God, and that you are not your own? For you have been bought with a price; therefore glorify God in your body. – 1 Corinthians 6:18-20

Prayer

Jehovah Lord, I ask for forgiveness; Heavenly Father, I am a sinner; I have sinned against You and my spouse. Lord Jesus, Satan and his agents are heavily using me. Deliver me from the hands of my oppressors. I know deep inside me the devil has been using me through spirits of pornography, ruling my life and marriage. Lord Jesus, help me; set me free because I am tired of Satan controlling my life and my marriage. The Lord God Almighty, I know You died on the cross of Calvary for my sins; I accept You as my personal savor and Lord. Heavenly Father, touch my life and destroy any filthy garment Satan has prepared for me. Lord Jesus, break me, mold me, and use me as You please. Deliver me from the hands of the wicked. Father Lord, take absolute control in every department in my life. I ask that Your thunder fire overwhelm every area in my life in Jesus' name.

1. I break loose from every spirit of pornography controlling my life in Jesus' name.

2. Father Lord, burn every lust in my eyes in the mighty name of Jesus Christ.

3. Jehovah Lord, close every doorway of lust that Satan is using to draw me closer to the kingdom of darkness in Jesus' name.

4. I bind and paralyze every spirit of pornography and spirit of masturbation challenging my life in Jesus' name.

5. I bind and paralyze every spirit of prostitution running riot in my life in Jesus' name.

6. Fire of God destroys every spirit of pornography using my life as a doormat in Jesus' name.

7. Every spirit associated with the spirits of pornography bargaining for my life catches the fire of God in Jesus' name.

8. Heavenly Father, deliver me by Your mighty power, and set me free from the hands of the wicked in Jesus' name.

9. I break every evil power over my life in Jesus' name.

10. I break every spirit of masturbation over my life in Jesus' name.

11. I break every spirit of pornography over my life in Jesus' name.

12. I break every spirit of bestiality over my life in Jesus' name.

13. I break every spirit of gender manipulation over my life in Jesus' name.

14. I break every spirit of rape over my life in Jesus' name.

15. I break every spirit of sexual perversion over my life in Jesus' name.

16. I break loose from every spirit of fornication in Jesus' name.

17. I break loose from every spirit of sexual immorality in Jesus' name.

18. I nullify every effect of sexual perversion upon my life in Jesus' name.

19. I divorce myself from every spirit husband in Jesus' name.

20. I divorce myself from every spirit wife in Jesus' name.

21. I bind and paralyze every evil stranger in my life in Jesus' name.

22. Holy Ghost fire purges my life, and sets me free from the spirits of pornography in Jesus' name.
23. Jehovah Lord, destroy every evil activity in my life by Your thunder fire in Jesus' name.
24. Lord Jesus, deliver me from the spirit of lust and perversion in Jesus' name.
25. Every spirit of spiritual husband controlling my sex life catches the fire of God in Jesus' name.
26. Every spirit of spiritual wife controlling my sex life, catch the fire of God in Jesus' name.
27. I break myself loose from every spirit of pornography in Jesus' name.
28. I set myself free from all spiritual pollution harassing my life in Jesus' name.
29. I bind and cancel every sexual immorality over my life in Jesus' name.
30. I destroy every power of sexual perversion bargaining for my life in Jesus' name.
31. I uproot every evil plantation of sexual perversion challenging my life. Come out and all your roots burn in the fire of God in Jesus' name.
32. Jehovah Lord, I thank You for delivering me from the spirits of pornography.
33. Amen.

You must command the evil spirits to leave you.

You must continue to rebuke them *seven times* by the power of the blood of Jesus Christ, and they will leave you completely alone in Jesus' name.

You evil spirits that cause me to be bound to the attacks of marriage killers, I renounce you and all your associate demons, and all your works in my life. I command you in the mighty name of Jesus Christ to lose your grip and release my marriage and me now by the thunder fire of God, in the matchless name of Jesus Christ I pray. Amen.

Chapter 6

I Am Leaving You

"I am leaving you."

"Why? Where are you going? Why are you leaving?"

"I just can't pretend everything is okay any longer; you and I know we fight every day, so why are we pretending everything is okay?"

"Sorry I have to go."

"But where? Where are you going?"

"I am going to live with my friend Gee."

"Why? Are you having an affair with her? No, you told me you two are just friends. But you are my husband—how can you go and live with another woman?"

"You know she is a caring person, she always listens to me, she always offers to sleep with me any time I want to do so, and we have lots of things in common."

~oOo~

"I am leaving you."

"What do you mean you are leaving? Where are you going?"

"I am going to live with my friend Mike."

"But you are my wife, so how can you go and live with another man?"

"I am sick and tired of the everyday fights; the abuse is too much. I am sorry but I can't keep up with your attitude any longer."

"Over my dead body! If you step out that door I'll kill you!"

"I can't live with you any longer."

"You mean you want a divorce?"

~oOo~

"I'm leaving you."

"Where are you going?"

"I am going to live with my girlfriend Saai."

"Why do you want to live with her?"

"She is caring and she loves me and I love her."

"What do you mean you love her?"

"All this time, I've been trying to tell you, but you wouldn't listen, and I can sense inside me that I'm not supposed to be with a man, as I have no feelings whatsoever for a man!"

~oOo~

"I am leaving you."

"Where are you going?"

"I am going to live with my friend Kilo."

"Why Kilo?"

"Because I love him, and honestly, I can feel inside me that I'm really not supposed to be with a woman."

~oOo~

"I am leaving you."

"What? Where are you going?"

"My boss at work has rented a place for me."

"But you are my wife, and we are still married."

"Not anymore."

"Why not?"

"Because I've been having an affair with my boss over five years now, ever since I started working there, and Susan is his child."

"What...?"

"He told me he is going to get divorced from his wife and marry me."

"Why does he want to divorce his wife and marry you? Do you even like him?"

"Yes, I do because he has changed my sex life ever since we met and I love him madly, as we have sex in his office almost every week."

~oOo~

"I am leaving you."

"Why are you leaving?"

"Because I don't love you any longer."

"Why?"

"I've been having a relationship with our neighbor's dog every night. I am even planning how I can adopt that pretty, sexy dog!"

~oOo~

Do any of these issues sound familiar to you or have you had conversations similar within your relationship?

There is a spirit specialized in destroying homes, marriages, and relationships. These spirits drive people to do many crazy things in life and usually target many loving homes and turn the life in that home upside down. Most of these homes are God-loving homes, spirit-filled Christian homes.

These evil spirits wait outside these godly homes for an opportunity to gain access into these homes.

If the targeted godly home is always on fire, meaning the prayer lives in such homes are intense, the assigned demon will remain stationed for a year or ten years because demons are very crafty and very patient. They wait until someone opens the opportunity – then they can enter such godly homes.

They can use a spirit of anger, spirit of bitterness, spirit of drug addiction, spirit of alcoholism, spirit of fornication, or spirit of pornography. Once any of these spirits get access inside such godly homes, all the associate spirits will then enter into such godly homes and start their work in various attacks. They focus on total destruction until their assignment is completed – then they move on to the next victim or assignment. The word of the Lord tells us:

The thief comes only to steal and kill and destroy; I came that they may have life, and have it abundantly. — John 10:10

For our struggle is not against flesh and blood, but against the rulers, against the powers, against the world forces of this darkness, against the spiritual forces of wickedness in the heavenly places. — Ephesians 6:12

As I said before, these spirits are called household wickedness, and they travel with multiple spirits such as spirit of divorce, spirit of abuse, spirit of financial hardship, spirit of joblessness, spirit of frustration, spirits of disappointments, spirits of anger, spirit of alcoholism, spirits of drug abuse, spirits of Jezebel, spirit of Prostitution, spirit of gender manipulation, spirit of bestiality, spirit of fornication, spirit of perversion, spirit wife, spirit husband, and many more spirits whose assignments are only to destroy homes and marriages.

I have heard many say something like this:

Reverend, I don't want a divorce—I'd really like to stay married, but I can sense inside me that something is driving me out of my marriage. The more I try to fix my marriage, the more these so-called forces are still controlling my spouse. What am I supposed to do?

You can intercede for your spouse to save your marriage. Consult with a healthy, balanced church minister, and seek deliverance and counseling. Or do a self-deliverance by following the principles of this spiritual warfare prayer book to set your marriage free from the hands of the wicked or from the hands of the spirits of household wickedness.

I have also heard questions such as these:

Is it okay for a man to leave his wife and live with his lover?

Is it okay for a woman to leave her husband and live with her lover?

No, it is not okay for a man or woman to leave their spouse for another lover.

Divorce is not the answer! Marriage vows are for better or for worse.

> "*For I hate divorce," says the Lord, the God of Israel, "and him who covers his garment with wrong", says the Lord of hosts. "So take heed to your spirit that you do not deal treacherously." – Malachi 2:16*
>
> "*Marriage is to be held in honor among all, and the marriage bed is to be undefiled; for fornicators and adulterers God will judge." – Hebrews 13:4*
>
> "*So they are no longer two, but one flesh. What therefore God has joined together let no man separate." – Matthew 19:6*

Turn around the issues in your marriage by calling in the name of Jesus Christ to rescue your marriage. As you pray this prayer in faith, our Heavenly Father God Almighty will pour His divine favor that will lift your marriage into the position of the head by turning the spirit of "I am leaving" into the spirit of "I am staying" over your marriage into Godly divine favor and perfection.

Prayer

Father Lord, I ask for forgiveness. God Almighty, forgive me of any sin I have sinned against Thee, and deliver me from the hands of the spirit of "I am leaving." Deep inside I know the devil has been using me through the spirits of problems, spirits of fighting, spirit of unfaithfulness, spirit of sexual perversion, spirit of gender confusion, spirit of alcoholism, spirit of drug abuse, spirits of anger, and spirits of bitterness. Lord Jesus, help me, set me free because I am tired of Satan controlling my life and my marriage.

God Almighty, I know You died on the cross of Calvary for my sins; I accept You as my personal Savior and Lord. Heavenly Father, touch my life, touch my spouse's life, and destroy any filthy garment Satan has prepared for us. Everlasting Redeemer, cause any satanic fountain overflowing my marriage to dry up right now in Jesus' name. Satanic rivers overflowing that flood my finances, dry up now in Jesus' name. Demonic overflowing river flooding my carrier, catch the fire of God and dry up now in Jesus' name. Rivers of satanic reservoirs overflowing in my family catch the fire of God and dry up now in Jesus' name. Father Lord, take absolute control in every department in my marriage and my life and heal me where I need healing, transform me where I need transformation, and deliver me where I need deliverance in Jesus' precious name, amen.

1. Lord Jesus, deliver my home from every spirit of "I am leaving," in the mighty name of Jesus Christ.
2. Everlasting Redeemer, every power of household wickedness controlling my home, destroy them all in Jesus' name.
3. Jehovah Lord, every power of sex addiction on assignment against my home destroy them all in Jesus' name.
4. I destroy every evil power eating away the love of my spouse to stay in our marriage in Jesus' name.
5. Evil strangers harassing my marriage, die in Jesus' name.
6. Blood of Jesus, Holy Ghost fire, pursue all strangers bargaining for my marriage into the Lake of Fire in Jesus' name.
7. Problems in my marriage that seem impossible to solve, fire of God take charge and take control of the situation in Jesus' name.
8. Heavenly Father, convict and deliver my spouse from the hands of evil seducers in Jesus' name.
9. Every agent of darkness toying with the mind of my spouse, hear the word of the Lord.
10. Angels of war, put frustration and disappointment upon the spirit of "I am leaving" that is bent upon destruction of my marriage in Jesus' name.
11. Powers of the spirit of "I am leaving" fueling problems into my marriage, die in Jesus' name.
12. Everlasting Father, let the angels of the living God pursue the spirit behind problems in my marriage in Jesus.

13. Armor of God, seal my spouse and me from every spirit of marriage destroyers in Jesus' name.

14. Favor of God shall pour my spouse and every area in my life to bring back our marriage into a godly marriage within a godly home in Jesus' name.

15. I refuse to allow Satan and the spirit of "I am leaving" to take over my spouse in Jesus' name.

16. Spirit of marriage destroyers on assignment against my home, collide with the Rock of Ages.

17. I break the power of every spirit of sex addiction challenging my marriage in Jesus' name.

18. I bind and paralyze you, every spirit of failure working in my home against my marriage, in Jesus' name.

19. Fire of God, set my spouse free from every evil attack of bondage in Jesus' name.

20. Jezebel spirit, controlling the organs of my spouse, dies right now in Jesus' name.

21. You, powers of the night destroying my marriage, die in Jesus' name.

22. I bind and destroy every demon in charge of "I am leaving you" in Jesus' name.

23. Satanic powers of "I am leaving you," your assignment is over in my marriage; die in Jesus' name.

24. Any evil powers of setback attacking my marriage die in Jesus' name.

25. Jehovah Lord, I thank You for answering my prayer in Jesus' name.

26. All cries of frustration and disappointments upon my marriage, bow to the power of God.

27. I arrest the arresters of my marriage in Jesus' name.

28. Lord Jesus, shine forth Your splendor into my marriage in Jesus' name.

29. I take back my marriage from the hands of the marriage destroyers in Jesus' name.

30. I reject bitter marriage. I claim testimonies upon my marriage in Jesus' name.
31. God of Elijah, send down your fire over my marriage, and destroy all evil strangers challenging my marriage in Jesus' name.
32. Father Lord, open every door closed to a healthy life and healthy marriage in Jesus' name.
33. Father Lord, give me extra love for my spouse in Jesus' name.
34. Fire of God, destroy every spirit of fornication, Jezebel spirit, spirit of gender confusion, and spirit of gender manipulation worrying my spouse's mind in Jesus' name.
35. Spirits of sex addiction running riot in my spouse's life die in Jesus' name.
36. Every habitation of cruelty fashioned against my spouse, become desolate in Jesus' name.
37. Lord Jesus, pour Your fire of love over my marriage in Jesus' name.
38. Powers of the night bargaining for my marriage perish in Jesus' name.
39. I shall love my spouse whether my enemies like it or not in Jesus' name.
40. I shall see the beauty of my spouse whether my enemies like it or not in Jesus' name.
41. I shall kiss my spouse with love and compassion whether our enemies like it or not in Jesus' name.
42. Father Lord, pour extra currents of love and affection over my marriage in Jesus' name.
43. Father Lord, give me extra affections and intimate cravings for my spouse in Jesus' name.
44. Heavenly Father, renew and restore every current of love that has died in my marriage in Jesus' name.
45. Every strange god on assignment against my marriage, scatter and die in Jesus' name.

46. Every power that has singled my marriage out for affliction, receive fire of God and die in Jesus' name.
47. Affliction shall never locate my doorstep in Jesus' name.
48. Affliction shall never locate my spouse in Jesus' name.
49. Affliction shall never locate my marriage in Jesus' name.
50. Ancestral witchcraft constricting my marriage, break loose and die in Jesus' name.
51. Powers of the night that are trying to turn back the clock of my life be broken and dismantled in Jesus' name.
52. Powers of failure against my marriage die in Jesus' name.
53. Arrows of darkness after my marriage, collide with the Rock of Ages.
54. Evil calendar of darkness for my life, catch the fire of God.
55. Satanic arrows fired against my marriage shall fall down and die in Jesus' name.
56. Evil weapon of shame to disgrace my marriage, lose your power now in Jesus.
57. Witchcraft agenda against my marriage, be destroyed now by the power of the blood of Jesus Christ.
58. Witchcraft chains used to hold my marriage stagnant, break into pieces in Jesus' name.
59. Jehovah Lord, let the extraordinary powers manifest in my marriage in Jesus' name.
60. Adversity shall never stand in my life in Jesus' name.
61. Adversity shall never stand in my marriage in Jesus' name.
62. Bondage against my marriage, hear the word of the Lord upon my marriage in Jesus' name.
63. Favor of God, rain upon my marriage in Jesus' name.
64. Marital peace, fall like refreshing showers over my marriage in Jesus' name.
65. I shall never give up; my problems shall give up in Jesus' name.

66. Fire of God, destroy the spirits of Jezebel in my marriage in Jesus' name.
67. Fire of God, destroy the spirits of fornication in my marriage in Jesus' name.
68. Fire of God, destroy the spirit of sexual perversion in my marriage in Jesus' name.
69. Fire of God, destroy the spirits of pornography in my marriage in Jesus' name.
70. Fire of God, destroy the spirits of anger in my marriage in Jesus' name.
71. Fire of God, destroy spirits of bitterness in my marriage in Jesus' name.
72. Fire of God, destroy spirits of setback and frustrations in my marriage in Jesus' name.
73. Others have failed in marriage, but with Your intervening love and grace my spouse and I shall succeed in the precious name of Jesus Christ.
74. Amen.

You must command the evil spirits to leave you.

You must continue to rebuke them *seven times* by the power of the blood of Jesus Christ, and they will leave you in Jesus' name.

You evil spirits that cause me to be bound to the attacks of "I am leaving," I renounce you and all your associate demons, such as Jezebel spirit, spirit of pornography, spirits of fornication, spirit of bestiality, spirit of perversion, spirit of gender manipulation, spirit husband and spirit wife, spirit of drug abuse, spirit of alcoholism, spirit of anger and bitterness, and all your works in my life, I command you in the mighty name of Jesus Christ to loosen your grip and release my marriage and me now by the thunder fire of God, in the matchless name of Jesus Christ I pray. Amen.

Chapter 7

Children of Divorce

"I want my daddy."

"My dad left home when I was five years old. I cried every night pleading for my dad to come back home."

"I missed my daddy."

"I ask my mommy when Daddy would be home."

"My mommy said Daddy is not coming home because he is living with his girlfriend."

"Why, Daddy"?

"Don't you love Mommy and me? Please come home, Daddy."

~oOo~

"I want my mommy.

"My mom left home when I was seven years old, and I ask my dad when Mommy would come home, and my dad kept saying Mommy went to work, but Mommy never came home."

"I really miss my mommy."

"Two months later, I saw a different mommy at home, but life wasn't the same because my mommy never came home. I really missed my mommy."

"I prayed to God for my mommy to come back home, but Mommy never came."

"I really love my mommy. Why did God allow my mommy to leave home?"

"If it is true that there is God, why did God allow my daddy to bring home another woman?"

"If it true that there is God, why did God allow my mommy to leave home?"

"Why me, God?"

~oOo~

The word of the Lord tells us that we should keep on praying all the time in the Spirit, with all prayer and supplication.

> *With all prayer and petition pray at all times in the Spirit, and with this in view, be on the alert with all perseverance and petition for all the saints.* – Ephesians 6:18

The Bible tells us to be rejoicing always, pray without ceasing, and give thanks to our creator God Almighty in all circumstances, either good or bad. He, Jehovah, is in control of any situation.

> *Rejoice always. Pray without ceasing. In everything give thanks* – 1 Thessalonians 5:16-18

Say the prayers below for your father or your mother or both of them if both desire to break up the home and marriage.

Prayer

The Father of the fatherless, I ask that You touch the life of my daddy, God Almighty. Let Your word sing, over, in, and through his heart piercing him to return home. Everlasting Redeemer, any strange power stealing the love of my daddy from home, cut them off so my daddy can come back home in Jesus' name.

Lord Jesus, touch the heart of my mommy so she can return home where she belongs in Jesus' precious name. Any strange powers stealing the love of my mommy, Jehovah Lord cut them off and release my mommy so she can come home in the mighty name of Jesus Christ.

1. Heavenly Father, take charge of my daddy's problems, and rearrange every situation that has been tampered by the agents of darkness in Jesus' name.
2. God Almighty, take total control of every issue my mommy is going through, turn that situation around, and let the solution prevail in the life of my mommy in Jesus' name.
3. Heavenly Father, renew the current of love upon my parents do not let them rest a bit of their minds without moving back home in Jesus' name.

4. Lord Jesus, I missed my daddy so much; please help him find his way home in the mighty name of Jesus Christ.

5. Everlasting Redeemer, home is not complete without my mommy; Jesus of Nazareth, please touch the heart of my mommy and help her find her way home in the mighty name of Jesus Christ.

6. Blood of Jesus Christ, escort my daddy home to his rightful place without any delays wherever he is in the precious name of Jesus Christ.

7. Power of the Holy Spirit, take absolute control of the life of my mommy, and escort her home to her rightful place without any delays, wherever she is right now, in the matchless name of Jesus Christ.

8. Heavenly Father, convict my parents, and let Your word pierce through their heart that they will renounce their unbelief's coming home together again in Jesus' mighty name.

9. Lord Jesus, Your word assures us that anything we ask in Your name You, Jehovah shall answer us; this moment I am pleading that You, Jehovah, intervene in the lives of my parents; whatever differences that has separated them from God of Isaac, God of Jacob, and God of Abraham, let Your will prevail in Jesus' precious name.

10. Father Lord, any evil act that has come upon my parents cursing them with divorce or separation, Heavenly Father, let Your blood intervene and let Your resolution prevail in Jesus' name.

11. Power of God and power of the Holy Spirit go to war on my behalf and bring my parents back home peacefully in Jesus' name.

12. Evil powers fueling confusion upon my parents' separation, bow to the power of God Almighty and be free from the lives of my parents' heart in Jesus' name.

13. By fire, by thunder of God, break through the heart of my parents and bring them back together again in Jesus' name.

14. Anytime my parents' name is mentioned for evil, Lord Jesus let my parents' names be attached with fire and consume those evils in Jesus' name.
15. I break every evil vow upon the separations over my parents in Jesus' name.
16. I break every power of setback attacking my parents. I renounce any powers of divorce and separation to release them now in the mighty name of Jesus Christ.
17. Barrenness of setback harassing the lives of my parents, backfire by fire.
18. I break the backbone of spirit of divorce upon my parents in Jesus' name.
19. I break the backbone of spirit of misunderstanding and spirit of confusion upon my parents in Jesus' name.
20. I break the backbone of evil powers eating up the love of my parents' marriage in Jesus' name.
21. I break the backbone of the power of the spirit of Jezebel interfering in my parents' marriage in Jesus' name.
22. I break the backbone of power of pornography causing the divorce of my parents in Jesus' name.
23. I break the backbone of the spirit of bestiality causing the divorce of my parents in Jesus' name.
24. I break the backbone of power of gender confusion cursing my parents into divorce in Jesus' name.
25. I break the backbone of every spirit wife cursing my parents into divorce in Jesus' name.
26. I break the backbone of every spirit husband cursing my parents into divorce in Jesus' name.
27. Fire of God, burn to ashes the ungodly things in the life of my daddy in Jesus' name, and the ungodly things that make him reject You, holy Father.
28. I set my daddy free from the hands of the wicked in Jesus' precious name.
29. I set my mommy free from the hands of the wicked in Jesus' precious name.

30. I cover my daddy with the blood of Jesus Christ.
31. I soak my daddy in the blood of Jesus Christ.
32. Blood of Jesus, shield my daddy in Jesus' name.
33. I cover my mommy with the blood of Jesus Christ.
34. I soak my mommy in the blood of Jesus Christ.
35. Blood of Jesus, shield my mommy in Jesus' name.
36. Blood of Jesus Christ restores the marriage of my parents in Jesus' name.
37. Fire of God, burn to ashes ungodly things in the life of my mommy in Jesus' name, and the ungodly things that make her reject You, holy Father.
38. Heavenly Father, I thank You for answering my prayer in Jesus' precious name.
39. Amen.

You must command the evil spirits to leave your home and your mother and father.

You must continue to rebuke them *seven times* by the power of the blood of Jesus Christ, and they will leave you in Jesus' name.

You evil spirits that cause me to be bound to the attacks of the spirits of divorce, I renounce you and all your associate demons, and all your works in my life; I command you in the mighty name of Jesus Christ to lose your grip and release my parent's marriage now; by the thunder fire of God, in the matchless name of Jesus Christ I pray. Amen.

Chapter 8

Depression and Marriage

When two individuals choose to form a marital union, that union is for better or for worse.

Depression causes a lot of tension and problems in marriages. Marriages with a disagreement or many arguments are likely to experience depression.

What are some causes of depression? It can be caused by traumatic circumstances in life such as the death of a loved one, a divorce in the family, unfaithfulness in the marriage, marital problems, personal traits, or sleep deprivation. Issues with addictions, such as alcohol, drugs, or perverted sexual behaviors affect the individual, and can also cause depression.

Others experience depression from financial failure, education, failing career, business, or lack of intimacy in the marriage. Depression, in general, is a very terrible thing to fight.

Sometimes you can sense there is something truly wrong within you that requires medical attention. However, in most cases, doctors cannot help you in your situation because it is a spiritual issue. The only solution is through prayer and deliverance to get Dr. Jesus Christ to take charge and take control of your situation to set you free from the hands of the wicked that are tormenting you.

> And the Lord said to him, "Get up and go to the street called Straight, and inquire at the house of Judas for a man from Tarsus named Saul, for he is praying." – Acts 9:11
>
> The steadfast of mind you will keep in perfect peace, because he trusts in you. – Isaiah 26:3

To grant those who mourn in Zion, giving them a garland instead of ashes, the oil of gladness instead of mourning, the mantle of praise instead of a spirit of fainting; so they will be called oaks of righteousness, the planting of the Lord, that He may be glorified. – Isaiah 61:3

Prayer

Heavenly Father, I ask that You touch me with Your healing hand. Everlasting Redeemer, any form of depression tormenting my marriage I bind and paralyze them in Jesus' name.

1. Jehovah Lord, I am a sinner, I ask for forgiveness; forgive all my sins in Jesus' name.
2. I resist and bind every spirit of depression in my life in Jesus' name.
3. I resist and bind every spirit of oppression and heaviness in Jesus' name
4. You, power of depression and anxieties over my life, lose your hold in Jesus' name.
5. I reject every spirit of oppression and depression over my marriage in Jesus' name.
6. Every power of discouragement tormenting my marriage, die in Jesus' name.
7. Every cause of depression in my life, catch the fire of God in Jesus' name.
8. Root of depression and oppressions over me, dry up now in Jesus' name.
9. Depression attacking my destiny backfires by fire.
10. I bind and paralyze every spirit of depression over my life in Jesus' name.
11. I claim deliverance from depression in my life now in Jesus' name.
12. I claim deliverance from oppression in my life in Jesus' name.
13. I claim deliverance from anxiety in my life in Jesus' name.
14. I claim deliverance from setbacks in my life in Jesus' name.

15. I claim deliverance from spirit of failure attacking my life in Jesus' name.
16. I claim deliverance of my marriage in Jesus' name.
17. I claim deliverance of my household in Jesus' name.
18. I bind and paralyze every spirit of the sea using my home as a satanic playground in Jesus' name.
19. I bind and paralyze every spirit of the land using my home as a satanic playground in Jesus' name.
20. I bind and paralyze every spirit of the air using my home as a satanic playground in Jesus' name.
21. I bind and paralyze every spirit of the tree using my home as a satanic playground in Jesus' name.
22. I cast out every power of depression and oppression from my life in Jesus' name.
23. I break loose from every evil chain in Jesus' name.
24. Evil powers militating against my life backfire by fire.
25. Powers of the night disturbing my mental health collide with the Rock of Ages.
26. You, spirit of household wickedness attacking my life, your assignment is over; catch the fire of God.
27. Holy Ghost fire, melt away every power of heaviness against my life in Jesus' name.
28. I cast out every spirit of depression and anxiety from my life in Jesus' name.
29. Holy Ghost fire, take control over my marriage in Jesus' name.
30. Holy Ghost fire, take charge, take control over every evil attack upon my life in Jesus' name.
31. I release myself from the spirit of depression and oppression in Jesus' name.
32. I refuse to follow evil commands over my marriage in Jesus' name.
33. I refuse to follow evil instruction over my mood in Jesus' name.

34. I bind and paralyze every mood swing challenging my life in Jesus' name.
35. I claim total deliverance from my mind, body, and soul in Jesus' name.
36. Blood of Jesus Christ, deliver me from the hands of the wicked in Jesus' name.
37. Father Lord, I thank You for answering my prayer in Jesus' name.
38. Amen.

You must command the evil spirits to leave you.

You must continue to rebuke them *seven times* by the power of the blood of Jesus Christ, and they will leave you in Jesus' name.

You evil spirits that cause me to be bound to the attacks of depression in my marriage, I renounce you and all your associate demons, and all your works in my life. I command you in the mighty name of Jesus Christ to lose your grip and release my marriage and me now by the thunder fire of God, in the matchless name of Jesus Christ I pray. Amen.

Chapter 9

Incubus and Succubus Spirit Husband and Spirit Wife

Incubus and Succubus are real, and they are sex demons of the night.

Incubus lies upon sleeping persons, especially women, with whom it seeks sexual intercourse. This spirit also blocks many single women in the spiritual realm from getting married. Sometimes, some single women can't find a husband. Men come into their lives only to use them and then leave. No man can stay in a relationship with them, and the more they try to find a life mate, the more they fail.

At some point, they tend to give up searching for a soul mate. Once these spirits have you in bondage, there is almost nothing you can do. You belong to it. Any man who is attracted to the woman in bondage to this Incubus—this evil destroyer, so-called husband—will frustrate the physical man that wants to build a relationship with the woman, or wants to marry her. This spirit will scare men away, through either dreams or physical manifestations. Sometimes the spirit husband will make the woman's face look like the face of a 130-year-old woman, smiling with no teeth, or it changes the face of the woman into an evil object that scares men off. For sure, no man will return back to her after such an encounter.

If this demon married you in the spirit realm, no one can marry you in the physical world. The demons marry you in dreams, and once this demon weds you, you will see yourself pregnant and giving birth to a spirit child. These evil children will follow you everywhere you go, because they are your spirit children.

If you have been having constant sexual intercourse in dreams without your consent, a spiritual husband has attacked you. The spirit husband has been using your body as a satanic playground.

I have delivered many marriages from spirit husbands and spirit wives' attacks. Some of the problems are so severe that the spiritual husband attacks the earthly wife. If the earthly husband becomes aware of the spirit husband having sex with his wife, the spirit husband becomes really jealous, violent, and starts choking the earthly husband, even to slamming the earthly husband against the walls.

Another tactic of the spirit husband is that it turns into a Succubus or spirit wife. It then starts having intercourse by force with the earthly husband in his dreams.

This demonic sexual attack on females may be caused by sexual sins, witchcraft spells, and curses of lust, inherited curses, or being a victim of sexual abuse. This demon can claim you while you are in the womb before you are born. True spells of witchcraft can attach these demons to most people, also having a one-night stand with a stranger who worships idols, or being in a relationship with someone with a serpentine spirit.

Succubus, spirit wife, is a demon in female form specialized in seducing men. Although feminine in meaning, in form this Medieval Latin word — Succubus — is masculine. It is a demon who specializes in sexual attacks on males. If you are having dreams or nightmares of a sexual nature that you know are as real as life, dreams where you cannot exactly distinguish the real from the unreal, demons are using your body.

There is a third demon called Mare, which works hand in hand with Incubus and Succubus. Mare causes dreams of sexual content coupled with those evil spirits. During the night, Mare sits on the chest and causes feelings of suffocation and choking, causing all sort of strange feelings of being paralyzed, and that its weight is crushing the breath out of you.

These demons have no respect for anyone.

Why is it that these evil spirits are allowed these to attack people?

Most attacks may be caused by sexual sins, witchcraft spells as well as curses of lust, inherited curses, pornography addictions, and being a victim of sexual abuse. These evil agents' assignments are to spoil marriages and to prevent singles from getting married physically, as they marry you by force in the spirit.

There are many people facing such terrible lifestyles keeping it to themselves, and never mentioning to their ministers that they face such issues in their lives. They never ask what to do about it.

These demons are primarily spirits of sexual perversion. They can get very violent. They often attack you by beating, restraining, and choking you. They are very abusive rapists, not sex partners, because they are taking and using your body for sexual intercourse by force.

These spirits cause overwhelming sexual urges in the body. They make it known that you have been attacked by demons. The sexual urges are so strong that they completely take over your mind and body. This can happen at any time, but usually while lying down.

If it happens, you cannot think about anything else, and it seems like you can do nothing to make the urges go away. It seems to you that the only relief for the urge is to have an orgasm by any means necessary. Once the spirit gets you sexually aroused or subdues you through violent sex, they begin to control your life. They will come in anytime and in some cases nightly violating and taking control of your sex life.

An encounter with an Incubus or Succubus spirit usually leaves victims feeling emotionally and spiritually drained because they steal their virtue. Most of the time, these evil spirits will impregnate you with their evil seeds of perversion and lust. Usually, the victim knows that these spirits want to control them, subdue them, and make them feel worthless. The experiences with these spirits are exceedingly intense so that sex becomes addictive in one's life. This induces guilt because of the pleasure your body experiences, and this pleasure lowers your resistance whenever they attack you.

Many powerful Christian men and women are going through such terrible sexual abuse in their lives against their will, and are ashamed to talk about it because they are not strong in their spiritual life. They are good Christians, but weak in their prayer life.

Is it true that a demon can rape a person?

You must allow them access into your body before they can do so, but yes, they can. Any type of disobedience can give demons access to your body for evil use. Individuals actively living in sexual sin constantly invite these demons into their lives.

Anyone in such bondage can be set free by following a simple spiritual exercise of praying and seeking deliverance from the hands of the wicked sex demons or night demons.

Here are some questions for serious consideration…

- Are you ready to be delivered from your present sexual encounters and other sexual sins?
- Do you frequently dream of having sex while sleeping?
- Is the agent of darkness using your body as a sex machine?

Satan and his demonic agents are evil…

The evil power of the night has an assignment to invade the body of the believer as well as the unbelievers.

If you know you should have been married by now, but for some unknown reasons you cannot find someone to marry, or you cannot stay engaged, seek a deliverance minister.

Many homes today are broken due to spirit husband and spirit wife attacks.

Many Christians ask, "How can I be set free from such demonic attacks?"

Whatever the devil has already done to you, now you have found Jesus Christ. He is in control of your body and soul. You will be lifted up to the height of purity, which God has created for you, only if you genuinely call upon His name to help you. Your only solution to such evil attacks is true deliverance.

You can seek a minister for deliverance or you can do a self-deliverance to be set free from such demonic bondage.

Open your Bible and read Leviticus 18:1-30. As you pray sincerely with a contrite repentant heart, the good Lord will set you free from the chains of sexual bondage from these evil spirits.

For the Lord of hosts has planned, and who can frustrate it?
And as for His stretched-out hand, who can turn it back?

– Isaiah 14:27

So they are no longer two, but one flesh. What therefore God has joined together let no man separate. – Matthew 19:6

And I will bless those who bless you, and the one who curses you I will curse. And in you all the families of the earth will be blessed. – Genesis 12:3

For if you are living according to the flesh, you must die, but if by the Spirit you are putting to death the deeds of the body, you will live. – Roman 8:13

Prayer

1. I deliver myself from the hands of the spirit husband and all evil seducers in Jesus' name.
2. I command all disappointment and embarrassment to bow to the power of God Almighty.
3. Evil spirit husband destroying my marriage, die in Jesus' name.
4. Evil spirit husband blocking me from getting married perish in Jesus' name.
5. Evil spirit wife destroying my marriage, die in Jesus' name.
6. Evil spirit wife blocking me of getting married, die in Jesus' name.
7. Powers of Incubus and Succubus tampering with my sex organs, catch thunder fire of God.
8. Any adult objects I ever played with in the past catch the fire of God in Jesus' name.

9. Ungodly things that comfort me while sleeping perish now in Jesus' name.
10. Evil garments in my life perish now in Jesus' name.
11. I ban and paralyze every power of the night in Jesus' name.
12. I recover my marriage from the hands of spirit husband in Jesus' name.
13. I withdraw my marriage from the hands of the wicked in Jesus' name.
14. Evil vows over my marriage are broken by the power of the blood of Jesus Christ.
15. Evil covenant over my marriage, be broken by the power of the blood of Jesus Christ.
16. Evil powers blocking me from getting married die in Jesus' name.
17. Power of the night selling my body, die in Jesus' name.
18. I renounce and denounce every agreement with this evil power in Jesus' name.
19. Blood of Jesus, rinse my sex organs and destroy every spirit husband that would try to penetrate in Jesus' name.
20. Evil powers bargaining for my body perish now in Jesus' name.
21. Evil spirit husband destroying my godly sex life, die now in Jesus' name.
22. Fire of God, encircle my life, and destroy every evil stranger around me in Jesus' name.
23. Fire of God, destroy every evil object in my life representing the demonic world in Jesus' name.
24. I break every evil soul's ties against my life in Jesus' name.
25. Evil mask over my face, catch the fire of God in Jesus' name.
26. Evil spirit husband following me around, expire now in Jesus' name.
27. Blood of Jesus, chase spirit husband out of my life in Jesus' name.
28. Blood of Jesus, cast all evil strangers in my life into the pit in Jesus' name.

29. Blood of Jesus, take charge of my life in Jesus' name.

30. Demons of Incubus attacking my marriage catch the fire of God in Jesus' name.

31. Demons of Succubus attacking my marriage catch the fire of God in Jesus' name.

32. Every demon of sexual addiction assigned over my life, I bind you permanently in Jesus' name.

33. Evil counselors against my marriage life, collapse in Jesus' name.

34. Heavenly Father, pull down and cast out every demonic stronghold built in my life by the spirits of Incubus and Succubus in Jesus' name.

35. I break the hold of any evil powers over my life in Jesus' name.

36. Powers of the night between my husband/wife and any strange man/woman catch the fire of God.

37. Demonic in-laws on assignment against my marriage, Oh God, arise with your righteous and holy anger and scatter them in Jesus' name.

38. Every decree issued against my marriage, I cancel now by the power of the blood of Jesus Christ.

39. I claim my deliverance from Incubus and Succubus' sexual immorality in Jesus' name.

40. I break every evil chain over my marriage in Jesus' name.

41. I release my marriage from the hands of the wicked in Jesus' name.

42. Thunder Fire of God, destroy anything ungodly over my marriage in Jesus' name.

43. Curses over my marriage, be broken and crumbled in Jesus' name.

44. Evil eyes monitoring my marriage, be blindfolded and lose track in Jesus' name.

45. Agent of the night bargaining for my marriage, Jehovah Lord destroys them without recognition in Jesus' name.

46. I move from bondage to liberty in Jesus in every area of my life, in Jesus' name.
47. Sword of God, destroy every evil agent tormenting my body in Jesus' name.
48. Lord Jesus, let Your power work mightily in every situation in my sex life in Jesus' name.
49. I destroy you, spirits of the night who work overtime against my sex life in Jesus' name.
50. Be broken every evil spell over my sexual appetite by the power of the blood of Jesus Christ.
51. Every satanic storm in my life is silenced permanently in Jesus' name.
52. Let the blood of Jesus pour deliverance over my life in Jesus' name.
53. Blood of Jesus, escort every demonic power controlling my sexual life to the Lake of Fire in Jesus' name.
54. I bind and paralyze all evil powers controlling and invading my sexual life in Jesus' name.
55. Fire of God, destroy every ungodly thing in my life in Jesus' name.
56. My flesh bows to the power of the Holy Ghost in Jesus' name.
57. Every trick of the devil over my life, be destroyed in Jesus' name.
58. Whether my enemies like it or not, I am set free from the bondage of the wicked in Jesus' name.
59. I disconnect my home, life, and family from every evil connection in Jesus' name.
60. Every evil desire perishes now in Jesus' name. All evil counseling, motivations, and plans I have received from the agent of darkness upon my life are destroyed right now in Jesus' name.
61. Stubborn problems pursuing me around are cut off in Jesus' name.
62. I reject every satanic judgment over my life in Jesus' name.

63. Let my life be filled with the holy fire of God, Heavenly Father, and destroy the evil spirits that are using my life as a playground in Jesus' name.

64. Lord Jesus, let every department of my life be filled with the holy fire of God to destroy any agent of darkness on assignment over my body in Jesus' name.

65. Holy Ghost fire, melt all over my body and take charge over my body in Jesus' name.

66. Everlasting Redeemer, I come into Your presence. Come into my life in Jesus' name.

67. Heavenly Father fills me with the Holy Spirit in Jesus' name.

68. This moment, this minute, this hour I command every demonic agent in my life to die in Jesus' name.

69. You, spirit of Incubus, I bind and cast you out of my life in Jesus' name.

70. You, spirit of Succubus, I bind and cast you out of my life in Jesus' name.

71. You, spirits of Incubi, I bind and cast you out of my life in Jesus' name.

72. You, spirits of Succubae, I bind and cast you out of my life in Jesus' name.

73. You, spirit of Eldonna, I bind and cast you out of my life in Jesus' name.

74. You, spirit of Eldora, I bind and cast you out of my life in Jesus' name.

75. You, spirit of Mare, I bind and cast you out of my life in Jesus' name.

76. Every associated sex demon in my life, your assignment is over; hear the word of the Lord in my life; die in Jesus' name.

77. Satan, you have no more control over my sex organs in Jesus' name.

78. Jehovah-Nissi, take charge over my sex organs in Jesus' name.

79. Heavenly Father, I thank You for saving my life in Jesus' name.

80. Amen.

You must command the evil spirits to leave you.

You must continue to rebuke them *seven times* by the power of the blood of Jesus Christ, and they will leave you in Jesus' name.

You, evil spirits that cause me to be bound to the attacks of marital barrenness, sexual dysfunction, misusing my sex organs, sex in dreams without my consent, evil mask of ugliness covering my face, blocking me from getting married, blocking me from a healthy marriage, blocking my sex life, blocking me conceiving beautiful children, causing me to be bound to sexual perversion, I renounce you and all your associate demons, and all your works in my life. I command you in the mighty name of Jesus Christ let loose your grip and release my marriage and me now, by the thunder fire of God, perish now in the matchless name of Jesus Christ I pray. Amen.

Chapter 10

Evil Spirit Children

Is it true there are evil spiritual children?

Yes, if the parent has encountered a spirit husband or spirit wife and been spiritually impregnated — yes, they will have evil spirit children around them everywhere they go. If the parent had these activities with the spirit spouse, and had a spirit child, they must destroy these evil spiritual children through spiritual warfare deliverance.

One can seek a deliverance minister or do a self-deliverance.

Use Scriptures against the demons, as they do not like to hear about the authority and power of the blood of the Jesus Christ, our God, and Heavenly Father.

> *Let the redeemed of the Lord say so, whom He has redeemed from the hand of the adversary.* – Psalm 107:2
>
> *In Him we have redemption through His blood, the forgiveness of our trespasses, according to the riches of His grace, which He lavished us in all wisdom and insight.* – Ephesians 1:7-8
>
> *The spirit of the Lord is upon me, because he anointed me to preach the gospel to the poor. He has sent me to proclaim release to the captives, and recovery of sight to the blind, to set free those who are oppressed.* – Luke 4:18
>
> *Behold, I have given you authority to tread on serpents and scorpions, and all the power of the enemy, and nothing will injure you. Nevertheless, do not rejoice in this, that the spirits are subject to you, but rejoice that your names are recorded in Heaven.* – Luke 10:19-20

Prayer

1. Holy Ghost fire, destroy every demonic child around me in Jesus' name.

2. Spirit of Incubus and Succubus children in my life, die in Jesus' name.

3. Fire of God, burn to ashes every unseen satanic child following me around in Jesus' name.

4. Everlasting Redeemer, make Your fire destroy every unseen evil object in my life in Jesus' name.

5. Strongmen children crying over my life, die in Jesus' name.

6. Children of the night following me around, perish now in Jesus' name.

7. I reject every satanic child in my life in Jesus' name.

8. Blood of Jesus, silence every demonic child crying and disturbing my peace in Jesus' name.

9. I disentangle myself from every demonic child attached to my life in Jesus' name.

10. Evil powers of the night using demonic children against me die in Jesus' name.

11. Evil spirit children militating against the divine purpose of my life, collide with the Rock of Ages in Jesus' name.

12. In the name of Jesus, I paralyze any and all evil children preventing my marriage.

13. Jehovah Lord, let Your thunder fire destroy all evil children standing against peace and unity over my marriage in Jesus' name.

14. Household wickedness tormenting my life with evil children, perish now in Jesus' name.

15. Spiritual husband and spiritual wife along with their children in my life receive the fire of God; perish in His flames of holiness.

16. Gadget of marital destruction using evil children against my marriage, crumble in Jesus' name.

17. Lord Jesus, let Your axe of fire cut every root of spiritual children upon my life into pieces, never to take root again in Jesus' name.
18. Everlasting Redeemer, redeem my life from the hands of the wicked in Jesus' name.
19. Jehovah Lord, let every satanic pregnancy in my marriage, and in the life of my husband/wife, be aborted now in Jesus' name.
20. I nullified evil desires, abortions, and miscarriages upon my life in Jesus' name.
21. Lord Jesus, deliver me from evil spirit children in Jesus' name.
22. Everlasting Father, I thank You for answering my prayer in Jesus' name.
23. Amen.

You must command the evil spirits to leave you.

You must continue to rebuke them *seven times* by the power of the blood of Jesus Christ, and they will leave you in Jesus' name.

You evil spirits that cause spiritual children to be bound to attack parental and marital issues, assigned demons in charge of using children against marriages, powers of the night, harassing my physical children to misbehave against my husband/wife and me, evil spirit children tormenting physical children in my life, demonic children living inside me causing me to disrespect my parents and adults, a spirit wife or spirit husband and demon children using me as a vessel against my parents, I renounce you and all your associate demons, and all your works in my life; I command you in the mighty name of Jesus Christ to lose your grip and release my marriage and me now; by the thunder fire of God, in the matchless name of Jesus Christ I pray. Amen.

Chapter 11

Demonic Attack over Your Marriage

There are many families whose marriages are under attack of enemies or evil powers. Some of these attacks are from our loved ones, friends, family members, in-laws, and neighbors who can't stand the marriage for whatever reason. Some of these evil attacks are from our previous intimate partners. Some are also from marital partners who are not God-fearing people, and instead practice evil activities that invite evil forces against their lives, against your life, and your marriage. Some partners lead a lifestyle that invites evil into their marriages. These partners are pursuing activities that are ungodly, and this disobedience invites demonic attachments.

Some attacks are from family members that do not agree with the marriage. As a result, they cast a spell on the marriage. If an in-law is against the marriage and causes an issue, sometimes he or she will do whatever it takes to destroy the marriage. The same holds true of parents and siblings.

Some attacks are from our friends that cannot stand the marriage, so they start causing all sorts of issues against the marriage. If the issue is a close friend who is jealous and who can't stand the progress of the marriage, he or she will do whatever it takes to destroy the marriage. Some family members or friends go to the extent of casting witchcraft spells against the marriage. Once the demons get hold of such marriages, they start instigating all sorts of issues such as financial hardship, unfaithfulness to the marriage, drug addictions, gambling, sexual perversions, and other equally vile problems to disintegrate the marriage.

Most of these evil or demonic attacks come with a price. These people believe the evil powers they call upon will protect them, but they are deceived because opening the door for the demons actually causes all kinds of problems for themselves, their families, and marriages as well as drawing the demons to your life and marriage.

Without a question, technology can be used by evil powers to destroy your marriage. Avoid unnecessary chat room visits as they can endanger your marriage. A cyberspace soul mate is not really a soul mate. You become emotionally attached to something in your imagination, but in reality, it is a computer screen. This emotional attachment leads to emotional detachment from your spouse. That is disobedience to God's order for marriage, and that can open a door to a spirit husband or spirit wife. Once evil spirits get a grip on your marriage, it is hard to make them let go because the assignment is to destroy the marriage before they leave you.

Infidelity doesn't always include sex. Emotional infidelity can breach marital trust and become debilitating to your marriage resulting in physical adultery. Stop sharing emotional closeness with someone of the opposite sex other than your spouse. The word of the Lord tells us that we should be of sober spirit, be alert. Your adversary, the devil, prowls around like a roaring lion, seeking someone to devour.

The word of the Lord is telling us that there is a force of darkness looking to cause you to fall. – 1 Peter 5:8

Learn how to protect your marriage through boundaries in the workplace. Protect your marriage by avoiding problem friends. They are not true friends, and can cause strife within your marriage. Protect your marriage through discretion in clothing. Most men are sexually aroused easily by the sight stimulation. What most women wear is very important. Attracting men through the kind of clothes you wear tends to defraud them because you cannot fulfill the desire you caused them to have. Avoid compromising games with the opposite sex outside of marriage.

So that at the name of Jesus every knee will bow, of those who are in Heaven and on Earth and under the Earth.

– Philippians 2:10

What are the things leading your marriage into failure? If you can name even two things, it is time to work hard at eradicating those things.

Prayer

1. Holy Ghost fire, destroy every demonic attack over my marriage without recognition in Jesus' name.
2. Demonic plotters against my marriage, Father Lord, expose them, let them lose track of me in Jesus' name.
3. I release my marriage from the hands of household wickedness in Jesus' name.
4. Evil powers fueling confusion in my marriage collide with the Rock of Ages in Jesus' name.
5. No enemy will use my marriage as a playground in Jesus' name.
6. Heavenly Father, let Your divine power rest upon my marriage in Jesus' name.
7. I claim goodness and favor of God over my marriage in Jesus' name.
8. Lord Jesus, let every situation work together for good over my marriage in Jesus' name.
9. I destroy every demonic attack upon my marriage in Jesus' name.
10. All evils holding hands over my marriage, Father Lord, scatter them in Jesus' name.
11. I resist every physical and spiritual being bargaining for my marriage in Jesus' name.
12. Jehovah Lord, I thank You for answered prayer in Jesus' name.
13. I receive knowledge and understanding over my marriage in Jesus' name.
14. In Jesus' name, I submit to the power of God over my marriage.

15. I overthrow every evil plan against my marriage in Jesus' name.
16. All my marital responsibilities that the evil spirits are controlling, I claim them back by the power of God Almighty in Jesus' name.
17. Every evil chain binding my marriage, break every link into multiple pieces in Jesus' name.
18. Host of Heaven, cooperate with my reconciliation in Jesus' name.
19. I reclaim tenfold all that the enemies have taken away from my marriage in Jesus' name.
20. Our God, Our Father, show me the divine breakthroughs into my marriage in Jesus' name.
21. Lord Jesus, breathe into every dead area in my marriage in Jesus' name, renew and restore it with living water.
22. Fire of God, burn every evil marital garment in my marriage in Jesus' name.
23. God Almighty, I invite the light of Jesus Christ to shine over my marriage in Jesus' name
24. I declare and decree the Holy Ghost fire to burn anything that belongs to Satan in my marriage to perish in Jesus' name.
25. Heavenly Father, I repent from all sins against my marriage in Jesus' name.
26. I bind and paralyze the strongman of deception and command all devouring spirits of lust to die in Jesus' name.
27. I declare my marriage holy to Jesus Christ, and invite the Holy Spirit to take charge take control over my marriage in Jesus' name.
28. I seal my marriage with the blood of Jesus Christ.
29. Jehovah Lord, I dedicate my spouse and my children into your hands in Jesus' name.
30. I break all evil bonds in my marriage in Jesus' name.
31. I break every remnant of the substance of disorder, disharmony, and disunity in my marriage in Jesus' name.

32. Jehovah Lord, I thank You for delivering my marriage from every demonic attack in Jesus' name.
33. Amen.

You must command the evil spirits to leave you.

You must continue to rebuke them *seven times* by the power of the blood of Jesus Christ, and they will leave you in Jesus' name.

You evil spirits that cause my marriage to be bound to demonic attacks, assigned demons in charge of my marriage destruction, powers of the night harassing my marriage, evil powers using my marriage as a satanic doormat, evil problems within my marriage, spirit of curses over my marriage, spirit of barrenness and childlessness over my marriage, Spirit Wife in charge of my marriage, Spirit Husband in charge of my marriage, demonic children living inside me causing my marriage's destruction, attacks from the demonic world on my marriage, I renounce you and all your associate demons, and all your works in my life; I command you in the mighty name of Jesus Christ to lose your grip and release my marriage and me now; by the thunder fire of God, in the matchless name of Jesus Christ I pray. Amen.

Chapter 12

Families Destroying Marriages

I believe my spouse's family may destroy our marriage since they do not approve of our marriage. Why is it my spouse's family always interferes in our marriage?

My wife's mother has been controlling, and I'm fed up with her and our marriage.

My husband's dad has been controlling, and I really don't know what to do anymore. How can I get him to listen to me instead of listening to his parents all the time?

What do I need to do for her to listen to me as a husband instead of always depending on her parents for advice? Why it is that the in-laws are always causing problems in our marriage?

My siblings don't agree with my marriage. They've been trying to break it up.

Why is it some families destroy their children's marriages? God did not intend for parents of the couple to control their children's marriages.

So they are no longer two, but one flesh. What therefore God has joined together let no man separate. – Matthew 19:6

For the Lord of hosts has planned, and who can frustrate it? And as for His stretched-out hand, who can turn it back?

– Isaiah 14:27

Prayer

1. Father Lord, I am in agreement with Your word in Mark 10:9, that what God has joined together, let no man put asunder to it in Jesus precious name.

2. I deliver my marriage from the hands of my in-laws in Jesus' name.
3. I deliver my marriage from the hands of my mother in-law in Jesus' name.
4. I deliver my marriage from the hands of my father in-law in Jesus' name.
5. I deliver my marriage from the hands of my parents in Jesus' name.
6. I deliver my marriage from the hands of my siblings in Jesus' name.
7. Any ungodly powers challenging my marriage, hear the word of the Lord in Jesus' name.
8. Family members on assignment to destroy my marriage, Lord Jesus, speak love, peace, and kindness into their hearts in Jesus' name.
9. Any family member that cannot stand my marriage, Holy Ghost fire, touch their life and bring peace and love within them toward my marriage in Jesus' name.
10. Father Lord, bring peace between my in-laws and my marriage in Jesus' name.
11. God of Heaven, let Your word pierce through the heart of my in-laws and let them accept me as I am in Jesus' name.
12. Jesus of Nazareth, bring peace between my in-laws and me in Jesus' name.
13. Lord Jesus, as much as I love my spouse, do not let my in-laws destroy our marriage in Jesus' name.
14. Father Lord, be the center of my marriage, and prevent family members that are trying to destroy my marriage in Jesus' name.
15. Jehovah Lord, I ask You in your mighty power to take charge, take control over my marriage in Jesus' name.
16. Father Lord, heal my marriage where it needs healing in Jesus' name.

17. Lord Jesus, transform my marriage where it needs transformation in Jesus' name.
18. Heavenly Father, deliver my marriage where it needs deliverance in Jesus' name.
19. Everlasting Redeemer, I thank You for making way for my marriage in Jesus' name where there was no way.
20. Holy Ghost fire, control my marriage from the hands of the wicked in Jesus' name.
21. Any ungodly power on assignment against my marriage collides with the Rock of Ages in Jesus' name.
22. Any familiar spirit challenging my marriage, bow to the word of the Lord in Jesus' name.
23. As the Lord lives, my marriage shall go on peacefully in Jesus' name.
24. Father Lord, bring my marriage out of extended family interference in Jesus' name.
25. Lord Jesus, intervene with my extended families that are against my marriage and let peace, joy, and understanding rain over their hearts in Jesus' name.
26. Father Lord, teach me how to acknowledge my parents peacefully without any arguments or problems concerning my marriage in Jesus' name.
27. Father Lord, teach me how to acknowledge my siblings peacefully without any fight or arguments concerning my marriage in Jesus' name.
28. Lord Jesus, teach me how to acknowledge my in-laws peacefully without any problems in Jesus' name.
29. Heavenly Father, teach my in-laws how to get along with my marriage and me in Jesus' name.
30. Father Lord, give me power and courage to communicate freely with my in-laws without any fear and pressure in Jesus' name.
31. Father Lord, I ask for peace to rain in my in-laws lives in Jesus' name.

32. Father, may the evil eyes monitoring my marriage be blindfolded in Jesus' name.
33. Jehovah Lord, I ask for Your mighty breakthroughs of peace and understanding between my-in-laws and me in Jesus' name.
34. Heavenly Father, I ask for Your mighty peace and understanding between my parents and my marriage in Jesus' name.
35. Everlasting Redeemer, I ask for breakthroughs of peace and understanding between my siblings and my marriage in Jesus' name.
36. Everlasting Redeemer, I thank You for taking control of any misunderstandings my in-laws, my parents, and my siblings' may have about my marriage in Jesus' name.
37. Thank You Jesus for answering to my prayer.
38. Amen.

You must command the evil spirits to leave you.

You must continue to rebuke them *seven times* by the power of the blood of Jesus Christ, and they will leave you in Jesus' name.

You evil spirits that cause my parents or in-laws to destroy my marriage bow to the word of the Lord; I bind and paralyze you in Jesus' name. You, demonic powers that are using my siblings against my marriage, perish now in Jesus' name. Satanic powers that are using my in-laws against my marriage perish now in Jesus' name. Satanic curse from my ex-friends challenging my marriage, perish now in Jesus' name. I renounce you and all your associate demons, and all your works in my life; I command you in the mighty name of Jesus Christ to lose your grip and release my marriage and me now by the thunder fire of God, in the matchless name of Jesus Christ I pray. Amen.

Chapter 13

Deliverance from Spirit of Masturbation

Masturbation is one of the most addicting activities that many struggle, with today. It has an intense affect, on hormone levels in our system, and affects our moods. This creates an addictive feeling. Some individuals focus on masturbation by watching pornography materials in order to have sex with their spouse. This is actually stealing from their spouse.

I have heard many complain about their problem, and these are some classic examples:

"Most of the time, my wife doesn't want to have sex — what am I supposed to do?"

"The more I try to quit, the more my eye and my mind begins to play games and tricks on me. I've been serving this spirit of masturbation for years. I really want to stop it, but the more I think of it, the more something within me pushes me to do it — so anybody, everybody, somebody help me stop such a sinful lifestyle! All my life, I've been a slave to it."

"Sometimes I will be minding my own business but I can sense something that somebody is telling me that it is time for pleasure, excitement. All I can see myself doing is running to my favorite secret place and start worshiping this sinful secret of mine, which is the power of masturbation."

"All I want is to stop it, so how can I stop it?"

"I did read the Bible; I see what the Bible says, but what does that have to do with my secret lifestyle? I'm not hurting anyone."

"How can I stop this secret lifestyle of mine?"

"I've tried to stop for many years, but the more I tried to stop, the more I failed, and the more I failed, the more I loved it."

There are many ways you can stop it completely.

The word of the Lord talks about immoral behavior.

Flee immorality. Every other sin that a man commits is outside the body, but the immoral man sins against his own body. Or do you not know that your body is a temple of the Holy Spirit who is in you, whom you have from God, and that you are not your own? – 1 Corinthians 6:18-19

Once you are married to a spirit of masturbation, you automatically sin against God.

Today, many people are automatically married to a spirit of masturbation without them even realizing it. Marriage initiated in the spirit realm is without the person's consent, but allowed by the person because of masturbation thoughts and activity.

I can hear you say, "So, Doctor, tell me more—I am really confused with this spirit of masturbation stuff." Let's take the questions one by one, and talk about them.

How can one be married to a spirit of masturbation in the spirit realm—is that even possible?

Yes, it is possible to be married to the spirit of masturbation without your consent in the spiritual realm by allowing permission in the flesh.

How does one give permission in the flesh?

Practicing such sinful acts from time to time gives these demons permission. As time goes on, you become addicted to it, and regularly practice it more often. There is a spirit that controls such behavior called Spirit of Masturbation, once you get deeper and deeper into it, the demon initiates you by marrying you without your consent in the spirit. This is how the spirits lay claim to you and your body, and it all takes place in the spiritual realms. One has no control over it, isn't even aware of it, during the ceremonies. But, you have given up your freedom from these spirits when you act in disobedience to God's will and to His ways.

When one seeks deliverance and renounces such evil spirits through the power of the blood of Jesus Christ, only then can the marriage be broken by force. Remember, the demons have no power against Jesus, the Son of God.

Most of the time, the demon will resist, and urge you to reject deliverance because all of them enjoy your company, and relish you being under their control.

How can a spirit of masturbation marry a living soul? What kinds of rituals take place during such marriage ceremonies without a person's consent?

The rituals are always a blood covenant that takes place in the spiritual realm between the individual and the spirit. Sometimes in dreams, sometimes while the person is in an unconscious state. Once one is addicted to the masturbation, you lose your strength of will, your freedom of choice, and it is as if your soul belongs to the spirit therefore it controls you and uses you as it wishes.

As you indicated that this type of marriage takes place in the spirit realm, does one have control to refuse marriage to a spirit of masturbation?

Yes. However, the only way, as I stated before, is to submit to the power of the blood of Jesus Christ. One must recognize the sin for what it is, agree with God that it is a sin, and seek deliverance from the spirit through blood of Jesus Christ. Then the marriage covenant will automatically be broken.

What kind of control and power does one have to free himself or herself from this spirit of masturbation? Can I divorce myself from this evil spirit of masturbation? Can I be set free?

The only control one has is by daily reading the word of the Lord, praying with it daily, and seeking deliverance. Bear in mind that once the covenant is broken, the spirit will be waiting patiently to come back. If one stops praying and reading the word of the Lord, the spirits will slowly reenter or come back home where they think they belong.

> "When an impure spirit comes out of a person, it goes through arid places seeking rest and does not find it. Then it says, 'I will return to the house I left.' When it arrives, it finds the house swept clean and put in order. Then it goes and takes seven other spirits more wicked than itself, and they go in and live there. And the final condition of that person is worse than the first." - Luke 11:24-26

The most effective way to be totally free of the evil spirits invading your life is to seek deliverance through Jesus Christ. The most effective way to stay completely free of the evil spirits is to replace disobedient behavior with obedient behavior to God. The most effective way to do that is to get close to Him through reading His word, praying His word, and submitting your will to His.

I know almost everybody does this kind of secret activity in their life sometimes, but is it really a spirit that controls this type of activity in human lives?

Yes, it is a spirit demon, Spirit of Masturbation.

This spirit travels with a group of demons such as spirit wife, spirit husband, spirit of prostitution, spirit of polygamy, and many more spirits that are destructive. Their assignment is to distract one from getting married physically. Therefore, these spirits will do whatever it takes to win you into their kingdom, and get you under their control. Their ultimate assignment is to destroy as many lives as they can in the earth.

No matter how many years this spirit of masturbation has been controlling your life, once you accept God Almighty, Jehovah, the Creator of Heaven and Earth will surely set you free. You must first ask Him for forgiveness, and then invite Him into your life.

Ask Him to take charge, ask Him to take control over every department in your life, and the same God of Isaac, Jacob, and Abraham will surely set you free. What He did for many, He is still doing today. He performs the wonders of setting captives or the tormented, lost souls free from the hands of the wicked.

The word of the Lord tells us in Genesis 2:24: *For this reason a man shall leave his father and his mother, and be joined to his wife; and they shall become one flesh.* Paul expounds on this truth:

> *The husband must fulfill his duty to his wife, and likewise also the wife to her husband. The wife does not have authority over her own body, but the husband does; and likewise also the husband does not have authority over his own body, but the wife does. Stop depriving one another, except by agreement for a time, so that you may devote yourselves to prayer, and come together again so that Satan will not tempt you because of your lack of self-control.* – 1 Corinthians 7:3-5
>
> *Let your fountain be blessed, and rejoice in the wife of your youth. As a loving hind and a graceful doe, let her breasts satisfy you at all times; be exhilarated always with her love.*
>
> – Proverbs 5:18-19

Prayer

Our God Our Father, I am a sinner with unclean lips; Jehovah Lord has mercy upon me. This moment I come unto Your presence, I ask for forgiveness. Any sin in my life that would hinder my prayer from being answered, Heavenly Father, forgive me in Jesus' name. Anyone I have sinned against that I do not know about, Lord Jesus, forgive me in Jesus' name. Amen.

1. Jehovah Lord, I come into Your presence through the power of the blood of Jesus Christ. I submit my life unto You that You take absolute control over every department in my life. I ask that Your thunder fire burn every sinful act and immorality in my life, make them burn into ashes in Jesus' name. Our God, our Redeemer, I take authority and renounce all sins and iniquities from my life. Every agent of darkness operating my life, I give

into the power of the Holy Ghost fire to destroy it in Jesus' name.

2. Evil powers that are on mission to destroy my life through spirits of masturbation, I command you to die in Jesus' name.

3. You power of the night tormenting my life, bow to the power of God in my life in Jesus' name.

4. I bind and paralyze every spirit of satanic rituals of voodoo, and of cursing spells, over my life, I cast you out into the Lake of Fire in Jesus' name.

5. I take authority over every spirit of masturbation and their associate demons controlling my life to perish in Jesus' name. You spirit of sexual perversion against my life, die in Jesus' name. You spirit of masturbation in my life, die in Jesus' name. You spirit of idolatry, fornication, disgrace, and witchcraft, get out of my life now in Jesus' name.

6. I break every ancestral curse following my family, my descendants, and me by the power of the blood of Jesus Christ in Jesus' name.

7. I bind and cast spirit of masturbation out of my life in Jesus' name.

8. I destroy every demon of masturbation upon my life by the power of the blood of Jesus Christ.

9. Holy Ghost fire, encircle my life and destroy every spirit of masturbation running riot in my life in Jesus' name.

10. I command evil spirits of masturbation in my life to be paralyzed and out of my life completely in Jesus' name.

11. Fire of God, remain permanent in my life, and burn to ashes every evil stranger in my life in Jesus' name.

12. Sexual perversion assigned against my life perishes now in Jesus' name.

13. I have received the cleansing fire of God in Jesus' name.

14. Lord Jesus, my Sacrifice, Oh God, I am broken with a broken and contrite heart God; deliver me from the hands of the destroyers in Jesus' name.

15. Everlasting Father, let Your Holy Ghost fire destroy every garment of sin in my life in Jesus' name.

16. Evil strangers assigned specifically to my life shall die in Jesus' name.

17. Every demon on assignment to destroy my destiny, all your designs shall backfire by the fire of God.

18. My providence, wherever you have been buried, be restored now by the power of the blood of Jesus Christ.

19. I raise the blood of Jesus Christ against every power of the night in Jesus' name.

20. I divorce myself from all spirits of masturbation by the power of the blood of Jesus Christ.

21. I renounce and cancel every evil vow over my life in Jesus' name.

22. I renounce and cancel every evil covenant over my life in Jesus' name.

23. I bind and paralyze all spirits of masturbation out of my life in Jesus' name.

24. I bind and paralyze all spirits of destruction out of my life in Jesus' name.

25. I bind and paralyze you spirits of seduction out of my life in Jesus' name.

26. I bind and paralyze you spirits of mind manipulations out of my life in Jesus' name.

27. I bind and paralyze you spirit of gender confusion out of my life in Jesus' name.

28. I bind and paralyze every evil spirit controlling my gender out of my life completely in Jesus' name.

29. Spirits of disgrace and embarrassment, your assignments are over in my life in Jesus' name.

30. Every agent of the night hovering over my life while I'm sleeping dies in Jesus' name.

31. Holy Ghost fire causes the fear of the Lord to camp around me, and scatter all evil strangers in my life in Jesus' name.
32. Jehovah Lord, I thank You for delivering me from the hands of the wicked in Jesus' name.
33. Amen.

You must command the evil spirits to leave you.

You must continue to rebuke them *seven times* by the power of the blood of Jesus Christ, and they will leave you in Jesus' name.

You evil spirits that cause me to be bound to the attacks of masturbation, I renounce you, and divorce myself from you, spirits of masturbation, and all your associate demons, and all your works in my life, I command you in the mighty name of Jesus Christ to lose your grip and release my marriage and me now; by the thunder fire of God, in the matchless name of Jesus Christ I pray. Amen.

Chapter 14

Sexual Relationships in Dreams

Why do some people have sex in dreams while sleeping?

Some people call it wet dreams.

There is a demon that performs seducing acts on people while sleeping. We've talked about them a lot in previous chapters. They're called Spirit Wife and Spirit Husband who perform sexual acts on people causing them to have orgasms while sleeping. Many people deny the possibility that these demons are real. But they are real! They are agents of Satan himself.

Demonic attachments can be so severe that people are attacked during the daytime while awake. These demons are having sex with them morning, noon, and night. This is a spiritual attack. If you encounter such attacks, you desperately need to seek deliverance immediately to be set free from such evil bondage. The sad thing is that too many people embrace the encounters thinking that if they can't get married, or their spouse won't give them what they sexually need then they may as well get it in dreams. This is a lie of Satan. Don't listen to it. Relationships with demons are sinful relationships. These evil spirits will not stop with just sexual encounters. They will invade your thoughts day and night, and will separate you from healthy relationships with human siblings in Christ. They will twist your thinking to where lies seem like truth, and truth seem like lies. Remember they serve the Father of Lies.

As you pray sincerely with a humble heart, the good Lord will set you free from the chains of sexual bondage with which these evil spirits are choking you.

The word of the Lord reminds us:

But immorality or any impurity or greed must not even be named among you, as is proper among saints.

– Ephesians 5:3

For the Lord of hosts has planned, and who can frustrate it? And as for His stretched-out hand, who can turn it back?

– Isaiah 14:27

And I will bless those who bless you, and the one who curses you I will curse. And in you all the families of the earth will be blessed. – Genesis 12:3

For if you are living according to the flesh, you must die; but if by the Spirit you are putting to death the deeds of the body, you will live. – Romans 8:13

Prayer

1. I deliver myself through the power of Jesus from the hands of the spirit husband and all evil seducers in Jesus' name.
2. I deliver myself through the power of Jesus from the hands of the spirit wife and all evil seducers in Jesus' name.
3. I command all disappointment and embarrassment to bow to the power of God Almighty.
4. Evil spirit husband or wife destroying my marriage die in Jesus' name.
5. Evil spirit husband/wife blocking me from getting married perishes in Jesus' name.
6. Any adult objects I ever played with in the past be consumed with the fire of God in Jesus' name.
7. Ungodly things that comfort me while sleeping perish now in Jesus' name.
8. Evil garment in my life perish now in Jesus' name.
9. I ban and paralyze every power of the night in Jesus' name.
10. I destroy sex demons in my dreams in Jesus' name.

11. I withdraw my life from the hands of the wicked in Jesus' name.
12. Evil vows over my life be broken by the power of the blood of Jesus Christ.
13. Evil covenant over my life be broken by the power of the blood of Jesus Christ.
14. Evil powers blocking me from getting married die in Jesus' name.
15. Powers of the night using and selling my body die right now in Jesus' name.
16. I renounce and denounce every agreement with any evil power in Jesus' name.
17. Blood of Jesus rinse my sex organs and destroy every spirit husband/wife that would try to use me while sleeping in Jesus' name.
18. Evil powers bargaining for my body perish now in Jesus' name.
19. Evil husband/wife destroying my sex organs die now in Jesus' name.
20. Fire of God, encircle my life, and destroy every evil stranger around me in Jesus' name.
21. Fires of God destroy every evil object in my life representing the demonic world in Jesus' name.
22. I break every evil tie that enslaves my life in Jesus' name.
23. Evil mask over my face catch the fire of God in Jesus' name.
24. Evil spirit husband/wife following me around expires now in Jesus' name.
25. Blood of Jesus hunt down every spirit husband/wife out of my life in Jesus' name.
26. Blood of Jesus, hunt down all evil strangers in my life in Jesus' name.
27. Blood of Jesus take charge of my life in Jesus' name.
28. Burn to ashes in the fire of God demons of spirit husband in Jesus' name.

29. Burn to ashes in the fire of God demons of spirit wife in Jesus' name.
30. Bind permanently every demon of sexual addiction assigned to destroy my life in Jesus' name.
31. Evil counselors against my life, collapse in Jesus' name.
32. Heavenly Father, let every demonic stronghold built in my life by spirit Husbands/Wives be pulled down in Jesus' name.
33. I break the hold of any evil powers over my life in Jesus' name.
34. Powers of the night attacking my life through the powers of the strangers catch the fire of God.
35. Oh God, arise with your anger and scatter all demonic agents on assignment against my life in Jesus' name.
36. Every decree issued against my life, I cancel now by the power of the blood of Jesus Christ.
37. I claim my deliverance from the spirit husband/wife sexual immorality in Jesus' name.
38. I break every evil chain over my life in Jesus' name.
39. I released my life from the hands of the wicked in Jesus' name.
40. The thunder Fire of God destroys any ungodly thing over my life in Jesus' name.
41. Curses over my life be broken and crumbled in Jesus' name.
42. Evil eyes monitoring my life be blindfolded and lose track of me in Jesus' name.
43. Jehovah Lord, destroy the agents of the night bargaining for my life in Jesus' name.
44. I move from bondage to liberty in every area of my life, in Jesus' name.
45. The sword of God will destroy every evil agent tormenting my body in Jesus' name.
46. Lord Jesus, let Your power work mightily in my sex life, and all situations in Jesus' name.

47. I destroy you spirit of the night working overtime against my sex life in Jesus' name.
48. Every evil spell over my sexual appetite be broken by the power of the blood of Jesus Christ.
49. Every satanic storm in my life be silenced permanently in Jesus' name.
50. Let the blood of Jesus speak deliverance over my life in Jesus' name.
51. Blood of Jesus escort every demonic power controlling my sexual life to the lake of fire in Jesus' name.
52. Heavenly Father, I thank You for delivering me from the hands of the wicked in Jesus' name.
53. Amen.

You must command the evil spirits to leave you.

You must continue to rebuke them *seven times* by the power of the blood of Jesus Christ, and they will leave you in Jesus' name.

You evil spirits that cause me to be bound to the attacks of sex addiction in dreams, I renounce you, and divorce myself from you. Spirits of sexual addiction in my dreams, and all your associate demons, such as spirit husband and spirit wife, and all your works in my life, I command you in the mighty name of Jesus Christ to lose your grip, and release my marriage and me now by the thunder fire of God, in the matchless name of Jesus Christ I pray. Amen.

Chapter 15

Marital Oppression

Why is it that Satan and his agents have many people oppressed and under his bondage? Why do so many allow him to oppress their marriage?

Oppression has become a big concern in the human race today. Many are suffering from financial oppression, carrier oppression, family oppression, social oppression, racial oppression, and handicap oppression.

Most of the time, these oppressions cause marital problems. However, marital oppression sometimes happens because one or the other spouse doesn't realize one can misuse power in the marriage. The power we are talking about here is within intimacy and domesticity in the marriage relationship.

Using excessive control over intimate moments or in daily living within the household causes many problems for both spouses. Communication comes to a halt, and accusations rise. In marriage, the submissive spouse has become an object or instrument by which the domineering spouse maintains a sense of control making life miserable for everyone. Withholding the intimate act of love from husband or wife in order to get one's way is manipulation and oppression. Refusing reasonable requests for help, or refusing to share the household responsibilities is a misuse of power.

There are natural issues that marriages go through such as conflict. Most marriages experience strong differences of opinion, arguments, and so forth! Spouses are sometimes unkind to each other. Spouses lose their tempers and can sometimes blow up at each other. These are part of tension and conflict that arise when imperfect men and women join lives together in marital relationships. It is normal.

Some married couples who experience normal conflict may require help from other sources to tone down the conflict. Some couples work through their differences by themselves within mutual love, consideration, and forgiveness. God is the ultimate marriage counselor, and a regimen of daily Bible readings and prayer will help strengthen all marriages. Marriage is a union; it takes two to make it happen, and God's help to seal it.

Marital abuse, however, is when there is always a one-sided, oppressive, manipulative, relationship. This is when one spouse establishes unhealthy control over the other by using tactics of abuse designed to get his or her own way. Some go to the extent that they will block their spouse from seeing family members or going out with friends. The husband demands the wife seek permission to call family, or to use the car for trips other than to the grocery store or taking the children to school. The wife may continually nag or harp to make the husband feel a call to a family member is not worth the contentions that the wife exerts. She may have a continual negative dialogue about her husband's character, manliness, abilities, and even sexual performances; all of it designed to bend the other spouse to the will of the one without regard for feelings.

> *If anyone is to go into captivity, into captivity he will go. If anyone is to be killed with the sword, with the sword he will be killed. This calls for patient endurance and faithfulness on the part of God's people.* – Revelation 13:10

Prayer

1. I bind every satanic attack over my life and marriage in Jesus' name.
2. Father Lord, deliver me from oppression in Jesus' name.
3. I command all satanic retaliation upon my marriage to fail in Jesus' name.

4. Marital oppressors over my marriage receive the stripes of fire in Jesus' name.

5. Demons gathering over my marriage be scattered in Jesus' name.

6. I break loose of all demonic oppressions upon my life in Jesus' name.

7. Legions working on my marriage receive fire of God in Jesus' name.

8. Witchcraft powers attacking my marriage, in Jesus' name, your sources of power are depleted.

9. I destroy every satanic mirror monitoring my marriage in Jesus' name.

10. Jehovah Lord, let Your light shine upon my marriage in Jesus' name.

11. Father Lord, please deliver my marriage from every confusion and frustration in Jesus' name.

12. Heavenly Father, pour joy, peace, and harmony from the open windows of Heaven upon my marriage in Jesus' name.

13. I bind and paralyze every pain and disappointment attacking my marriage in Jesus' name.

14. Spiritual powers harassing my married life be smitten with blindness in Jesus' name.

15. My enemies shall never prevail over my marriage in Jesus' name.

16. Terrors of the night bargaining for my marriage receive the sword of God Almighty.

17. Evil seed of the enemy planted in my marriage be uprooted in Jesus' name.

18. Holy Ghost, burn and destroy every stranger of the night attacking my marriage in Jesus' name.

19. Powers of the oppressors challenging God in my marriage collide with the Rock of Ages in Jesus' name.

20. I shall not give up; in Jesus' name, the problems in my marriage shall give up.

21. Trouble upon my marriage cease now in Jesus' name.

22. God, arise and fight for my spouse and me in Jesus' name.
23. God, arise on my behalf and challenge my oppressors in Jesus' name.
24. Heavenly Father, put my oppressors to shame in Jesus' name.
25. Father Lord, turn all evil curses upon my marriage into blessings in Jesus' name.
26. Heavenly Father, deliver my marriage from the hands of the wicked in Jesus' name.
27. Vultures eating up love in my marriage your stomachs are sour, and your throat closes up right now in Jesus' name.
28. Foundational bondage attacking my marriage bow to the power of God Almighty in Jesus' name.
29. Ancestral bondage attacking my marriage bow to the power of God Almighty in Jesus' name.
30. Every evil agent assigned and working overtime to destroy my marriage dies in Jesus' name.
31. Lord God, quench now every strange fire prepared by the witches over my marriage in Jesus' name.
32. Ancestral idols fighting over my life be destroyed now in Jesus' name.
33. Ancestral demons fighting over my marriage be destroyed now in Jesus' name.
34. Fire of God arise and fight for my family in Jesus' name.
35. Ancestral curse of idolatry in my foundation die in Jesus' name.
36. Parental curse of frustration in my foundation be broken by the power of the blood of Jesus Christ.
37. Failure prepared for my life turn into divine blessings in Jesus' name.
38. Covenant with witchcraft spirits, family gods, and spirit husband and spirit wife be broken by the power of the blood of Jesus Christ.
39. No family idol powers shall prevail over my family in Jesus' name.

40. Evil altars where my marital pictures are kept catch the fire from God now in Jesus' name.
41. I shall rejoice in marital favor and blessings in Jesus' name.
42. Father Lord, I thank You for delivering my marriage from the hands of the oppressors in Jesus' name. Amen.

You must command the evil spirits to leave you.

You must continue to rebuke them *seven times* by the power of the blood of Jesus Christ, and they will leave you in Jesus' name.

You evil spirits that cause me to be bound to the attacks of marital oppression, I renounce you and all your associate demons, and all your works in my life; I command you in the mighty name of Jesus Christ to lose your grip and release my marriage and me now by the thunder fire of God, in the matchless name of Jesus Christ I pray. Amen.

Chapter 16

Destroying the Destroyer of Your Marriage

Christians, enough is enough — it is time for us to use the authority God Almighty gave us to destroy these destroyers, these spirits of destruction.

> *Behold, I have given you authority to tread on serpents and scorpions, and over all the power of the enemy, and nothing will injure you.* – Luke 10:19
>
> *You will also decree a thing, and it will be established for you; and light will shine on your ways.* – Job 22:28

Prayer

1. I bind and paralyze every power of the spirit called Destroyer in Jesus' name.
2. I shall never bow to the spirits of destruction in Jesus' name.
3. Every foundational bondage that is attacking my providence breaks now in Jesus' name.
4. Roast evil instrument of destruction fashioned against my marriage, in Jesus' name.
5. I command all foundation demons attacking my marriage to die in Jesus' name.
6. Piercing fire of God destroys every foundational bondage against my life and marriage in Jesus' name.
7. Satanic walls of destruction fashioned against my marriage receive the thunder fire of God.
8. Jehovah Lord, let the thunder fire of God scatter all evil strangers in my life in Jesus' name.

9. Every gate open to my oppressors is sealed now by the power of the blood of Jesus Christ.

10. Foundational destroyers manifesting frustration and disappointment in my marriage shall be canceled now in Jesus' name.

11. Spirit of disappointments challenging my marriage, die in Jesus' name.

12. Spirit of confusion challenging my marriage, die in Jesus' name.

13. Spirit of frustration challenging my marriage, die in Jesus' name.

14. Spirit of anger challenging my marriage, die in Jesus' name.

15. Spirit of bitterness challenging my marriage, die in Jesus' name.

16. Spirit of problems pouring problems into my marriage, die in Jesus' name.

17. Spirit of disgrace pouring disgrace into my marriage, die in Jesus' name.

18. Spirit of gender manipulation harassing the sex life in my marriage, die in Jesus' name.

19. Spirit of bestiality challenging my marriage die in Jesus' name.

20. Spirit of pornography challenging my marriage, die in Jesus' name.

21. Spirit of sexual perversion challenging my marriage, die in Jesus' name.

22. Spirit of prostitution challenging my marriage, die in Jesus' name.

23. Spirit of gender disorder interfering in my marriage, die in Jesus' name.

24. Satanic covenant strengthening the foundation of any bondage against my life, be broken in Jesus' name.

25. Every chain of helplessness binding my marriage breaks now in Jesus' name.

26. I decree divine favor upon my marriage in Jesus' name.
27. I bind and destroy every yoke of the enemy upon my marriage in Jesus' name.
28. I bind and paralyze all anti-miracle witches in my life in Jesus' name.
29. I bind and paralyze all anti-miracle wizards in my marriage in Jesus' name.
30. I retrieve my marriage from the hands of the wicked in Jesus' name.
31. I retrieve my spouse from the hands of the destroyer by the power of the blood of Jesus Christ.
32. Holy Host fire burns to ashes every stranger of the night attacking my spouse in Jesus' name.
33. Holy Ghost fire burns to ashes every spirit of destruction challenging my marriage in Jesus' name.
34. Father Lord, wipe away my tears and give rain of joy to soak my life in Jesus' name.
35. Father Lord, wipe away my tears and let the rain of peace rain in my life in Jesus' name.
36. Father Lord, wipe away my tears and let the rain of happiness soak my life in Jesus' name.
37. Jehovah Lord, I reject the anointing of non-achievement against me in Jesus' name.
38. My life shall move forward in goodness and mercy whether my enemies like it or not in Jesus' name.
39. I shall rejoice and praise the name of the Lord in Jesus' name.
40. Jehovah Lord, I thank You for the deliverance from destroying spirits in my marriage in Jesus' name.
41. Amen.

You must command the evil spirits to leave you.

You must continue to rebuke them *seven times* by the power of the blood of Jesus Christ, and they will leave you in Jesus' name.

You evil spirits that cause me to be bound by the attacks destroying my marriage, I destroy you and all of your destroyers attacking my marriage by the power of the blood of Jesus Christ. I renounce you and all your associate demons, and all your works in my life; I command you in the mighty name of Jesus Christ to lose your grip and release my marriage and me now by the thunder fire of God, in the matchless name of Jesus Christ I pray. Amen.

Chapter 17

The Attack of the Jezebel Spirit

Who is this Spirit of Jezebel that gets into every man's business? Is it true she destroys marriages? It is true she actually confuses many ministers so that they tend to forget what they need to preach about? Is it true that she holds the power over many lives?

Who is this Jezebel spirit? How come she is so powerful? Where did she come from? Is it true she charms many men with seduction?

Why does she frustrate and destroy so many marriages? How is she able to seduce both married and single men as her slaves? How can we get rid of her? Is it true she is in every church? Can this spirit get into Christians? Does she only come from satanic worship?

Let's hear what the word of the Lord says about the spirit of Jezebel.

But I have this against you, that you tolerate the woman Jezebel, who calls herself a prophetess, and she teaches and leads my bondservants astray so that they commit acts of immorality and eat things sacrificed to idols. I gave her time to repent, and she does not want to repent of her immorality. Behold, I will throw her on a bed of sickness and those who commit adultery with her into great tribulation, unless they repent of her deeds. And I will kill her children with pestilence, and all the churches will know that I am He who searches the minds and hearts; and I will give to each one of you according to your deeds. – Revelation 2:20-23

Jezebel uses tools of manipulation, intimidation, and domination against men.

She is very good at wearing flashy clothes—clothes that get attention. Today she has many agents that follow her steps in many churches, causing all sorts of problems, confusion, and sexual attention. Her clothes confuse men at church, turning many churches today into a satanic playground. The agents will come to your church with one agenda: they will first attack the minister with flashy, short skirts, confusing the worship and trying to overthrow the worship of God. Many ministers have accidentally fallen under the domination of Jezebel allowing Jezebel to control the church.

The spirits of Jezebel are very powerful, and should be taboo in churches. They will come to the minister for counseling with almost no clothes on, and make sure they sit in such a way that the minister will lose track of the theme being addressed. She is specialized as a seductress, adulteress, fornicator, and in perverted sexual lifestyle that controls many married and single men. She is worse than a home wrecker and a home destroyer because she invades the minds and hearts of men and women specifically to destroy godly relationships. I've seen many powerful evil spirits destroying homes, but nothing like Jezebel. She actually comes with a master plan full of surprises.

> *Because His judgments are true and righteous, for He has judged the great harlot who was corrupting the Earth with her immortality, and He has avenged the blood of His bondservants on her.* – Revelation 19:2

Jezebel calls herself a prophetess according to the Holy Bible, but she is a false prophetess. Jezebel is a seducer; she seduces others into spiritual fornication with her. She pronounces a false doctrine that is pleasing to the people's ear, tickling their ears with half-truths. Jezebel was a liar, and the spirit called after her name is no different. She weaves just enough truth into a doctrine to make it sound right when it is actually full of lies aimed at deception and division.

This Jezebel spirit is never satisfied with what she has. She always demands gratification and to be fawned over. She always offers her body and love on everything around her.

> *Do you not know that your bodies are members of Christ? Shall I then take away the members of Christ and make them members of a prostitute? Mat it never be! Or do you not know that the one who joins himself to a prostitute is one body with*

her? For He says, "The two shall become one flesh." But the one who joins himself to the Lord is one spirit with Him.

– 1 Corinthians 6:15-17

Jezebel loves to glorify herself. This demon causes many women to be miserable, clueless, and unrepentant. The women controlled by this spirit live a sensuous lifestyle never caring about the men they seduce or the homes they destroy.

To the degree that she glorified herself and lived sensuously, to the same degree give her torment and mourning; for she says in her heart, "I sit as a queen and I am not a widow, and will never see mourning." – Revelation 18:7

Now, then, hear this, you sensual one, who dwells securely, who says in your heart, "I am, and there is no one besides me. I will not sit as a widow, nor know loss of children."

– Isaiah 47:8

Because you say, I am rich, and have become wealthy, and have need of nothing, and you do not know that you are wretched and miserable and poor and blind and naked.

– Revelation 3:17

Any outside force controls no one unless he or she allows it. The problem is that many men allow lust to pervade their thoughts, and the spirit of lust has a grip on their lives. For example, once they enter into their secret places where no one is watching, they begin to watch pornographic movies, Internet porn videos, and viewing pornographic magazines. This causes increases feelings of lust opens the door to seduction, and it leads them astray. They have given power to the spirits of Jezebel to control their lives.

Jezebel spirit cannot deceive you without seducing you first. She travels with many associate spirits such as Lust, Seduction, Fornication, Sexual Perversion, Gender Manipulation, Prostitution and Unnatural Sexual Urges, Error, and the spirits of witchcraft addiction and bondage.

If a man is not spiritually sound, these evil spirits will start playing tricks and games in his mind, making him think he needs something special that his spouse or girlfriend doesn't have, and this leads him into destruction. Each and every one of these spirits is a home wrecker, specializing in giving you infirmities and crippling your marriage or your relationships.

Many powerful men, presidents of many businesses, organizations, high priests, and elders and leaders of the church all have been under the skirt of Jezebel. Many are trying to leave the Jezebel lifestyle, but the spirit is so powerful that the more they try to leave, the more they get introduced to a new agent of Jezebel with a different approach making it impossible to be set free.

I pray that no matter how deep of a pit you are in, no matter how deep under Jezebel's domination, today by the power of the blood of Jesus Christ, you will be set free in Jesus' name. Amen.

> *To deliver you from the strange woman, from the adulteress who flatters with her words...* – Proverbs 2:16
>
> *For the lips of an adulteress drip honey and smoother than oil is her speech...* – Proverbs 5:3
>
> *For why should you, my son, be exhilarated with an adulteress and embrace the bosom of a foreigner?* – Proverbs 5:20
>
> *To keep you from the evil woman, from the smooth tongue of the adulteress ...* – Proverbs 6:24

Prayer

Lord Jesus, I ask for forgiveness. Heavenly Father, I am a sinner, I have sinned against Thee.

Jehovah Lord, forgive and deliver me from the hands of the oppressors. I know deep inside me the Jezebel spirits and all associates are using me through spirits of sexual perversion. Lord Jesus, help me, set me free. I am tired of Satan controlling my life and marriage. Jesus of Nazareth, I know You died on the cross of Calvary for my sins. I accept You as my personal Savior and Lord. Heavenly Father, touch my life and destroy any filthy, satanic activities in my life. Lord Jesus, take absolute control over every department in my life. Father Lord, deliver me from the hands of the spirits of Jezebel and all the rest of these wicked demons in Jesus' name. Amen.

1. Every associate demon of Jezebel harassing my life, die in Jesus' name.
2. All curses of Jezebel spirit and her demons attacking my life break by the power of the blood of Jesus Christ.
3. I bind and cancel every plan of Jezebel's over my life in Jesus' name.
4. Break loose, all spirit of Jezebel's attacks in any department in my life, in Jesus' name.
5. Spirit of Jezebel's influence manifesting in my life, I cancel your activities now by the power of the blood of Jesus Christ.
6. My soul ties with the evil spirit of Jezebel break loose in Jesus' name.
7. Spirit of Jezebel's seeds in my life come out with your entire roots in Jesus' name.
8. Powers of Jezebel controlling my life die in Jesus' name.
9. Holy Ghost fire, burn to ashes every spirit of Jezebel's activity operating over my heart in Jesus' name.
10. I bind and cancel every spirit of seduction attacking my life in Jesus' name.
11. I bind and cancel every spirit of sexual perversion attacking my life in Jesus' name.
12. I bind and cancel every spirit of sexual addiction operating in my life in Jesus' name.
13. I rinse my eyes with the blood of Jesus Christ against desires leading me into ungodly troubles in Jesus' name.
14. Associate demons of Jezebel following me around die in Jesus' name.
15. Every vow of Jezebel spirit over my life I cancel it now in Jesus' name.
16. Every covenant of Jezebel over my life, I break and cancel it now in Jesus' name.
17. Sex demons playing games in my sex life die in Jesus' name.

18. Spirit of sexual perversion attacking my soul lose your hold over me in Jesus' name.

19. Blood of Jesus Christ destroy every seed of Jezebel operating within me in Jesus' name.

20. Evil plantation of sexual riot inside me come out with your entire roots in Jesus' name.

21. Sexual urges running riot in my blood come out of me completely in Jesus' name.

22. I stand with the power of God against every power of sex addiction challenging my life in Jesus' name.

23. Every strange power controlling my life catches the fire of God.

24. Every strange power controlling my spouse catches the fire of God.

25. Lion of Judah, pursue and destroy every Jezebel spirit destroying my marriage in Jesus' name.

26. Fire of God scatters the sex demons away from my life in Jesus' name.

27. Fire of God scatter sex demons away from my spouse's life in Jesus' name.

28. Father Lord, let every manifestation of hindrance upon my life be departed in Jesus' name.

29. Demons crushing the relationship between my spouse and me be rendered powerless in Jesus' name.

30. God of a new beginning begin a new thing in my life in Jesus' name.

31. God of a new beginning begin a new thing in my marriage in Jesus' name.

32. God Almighty, create a wall of fire between spirit husband and spirit wife in my marriage in Jesus' name.

33. Heavenly Father, locate and destroy household wickedness controlling my marriage in Jesus' name.

34. Every blood covenant between spirits of Jezebel and me break now by the power of the blood of Jesus Christ.

35. Every vow made between the spirits of household wickedness and me break now by the power of the blood of Jesus Christ.

36. Evil vow between my spouse and the sex demons break now by the power of the blood of Jesus Christ.

37. All covenants made over my marriage by the spirits of destruction break now in Jesus' name.

38. Everlasting Redeemer, speak for me and answer all powers asking where my God is.

39. Jehovah Yahweh, I paralyze all marriage destroyers and the anti-marriage forces in Jesus' name.

40. Lord Jesus, let every demon's bands of bondage be removed from my marriage completely in the matchless name of our Lord Jesus Christ

41. Spirit of alcoholism leading me into Jezebel's kingdom, catch the fire of God in Jesus' name.

42. Every trap of Jezebel calling my name, backfire and perish in God's holy fire.

43. Demons of Jezebel bargaining for my life die in Jesus' name.

44. I break every spell of Jezebel over my life in Jesus' name.

45. Jezebel spirit within me leading me into destruction wherever I go, die now in Jesus' name.

46. My life anchors to the Glory of God in Jesus' name.

47. Fire of God, burn everything of no God within me into ashes in Jesus' name.

48. Fire of God destroys every sexual urge following me around in Jesus' name.

49. Jehovah Lord, I thank You for the deliverance of delivering me from the hands of Jezebel spirit and her demons in Jesus' name.

50. Amen.

You must command the evil spirits to leave you.

You must continue to rebuke them *seven times* by the power of the blood of Jesus Christ, and they will leave you in Jesus' name.

You evil spirits that cause me to be bound to the attacks of destroying my marriage, I destroy you and all of your destroyers over my marriage, by the power of the blood of Jesus Christ. I renounce you and all your associate demons, and all your works in my life; I command you in the mighty name of Jesus Christ to lose your grip and release my marriage and me now by the thunder fire of God, in the matchless name of Jesus Christ I pray. Amen.

Chapter 18

Destroying the Spirit of Polygamy

Why is it so many people are into polygamy today? The practice has invaded the television arena shooting waves of evil into American homes. Practicing polygamy violates God's specific design for marriage. God set marriage as a pure and private affair between one husband and one wife together in love and unity for a lifetime.

People sometimes wonder how this kind of demon can cause havoc in men's lives. If your father belongs to a cult and practices polygamy, and if for any reason he happens to pray for you — while you were a child, or adult at your wedding, or any other ceremony — then he lays hands upon you in prayer, the evil powers of going after multiple women will descend upon you.

If you are cursed with the spirits of polygamy, you are running after strange women all the time. Your ambition is to gather various women into your life, woman after woman, and lust drives you. You are acutely aware of any woman that passes by you. All you feel is your blood running riot within you craving women.

God's plans for marriage are forever. Only death should break a covenant between husband and wife. However, unseen forces seek to break such covenants. These demons go by many names including Jezebel, and they operate by planting evil deeds and destruction in marriages.

Such devious evil destroyers operate on promiscuity by either spouse such as spirits of prostitution, spirits of gender confusion, spirit of threesome, spirits of polygamy, spirits of household wickedness, and spirit of bestiality attack marriages in multiple forces.

Let's hear what the word of the Lord says about it.

You shall not commit adultery. – Exodus 20:14

And I will put enmity between you and the woman, and between your seed and her seed; he shall bruise you on the head, and you shall bruise him on the heel. – Genesis 3:15

Prayer

In the mighty name of Jesus Christ, I bind and paralyze every spirit of polygamy controlling my life. I reject and break every link with the kingdom of darkness through parental curses of polygamy relationships. I command destruction upon the spirit of polygamy defiling my life.

Every covenant that is binding powers of polygamy to my life shall be broken now in Jesus' name. Ancestral curses placed upon my life and upon my marriage be broken. All powers of the spirits of polygamy lose your grip. I set on fire evil spirit claims, marriage certificates, wedding rings, gowns, and all gifts. Polygamy children in my life catch the fire from God.

I command all witches, enchanters, polygamy spirits, divination, Jezebel spirits, addiction powers, and spiritual marriages against me to be destroyed by the powers of the blood of Jesus Christ.

I confess and receive a divine release from every yoke and bondage of the devil, spirits of polygamy, spirits of fornication, spirits of gender manipulation, spirits of gender control, spirits of sex addiction, spirits of sexual perversion, spirits of household wickedness, spirits of failure, spirits of destruction, spirits of infirmities, spirit wife and spirit husband. I shield and seal my life with the power of the blood of Jesus Christ. I accept restoration and renewal from God Almighty.

1. Power of the night fueling polygamy in my marriage die in Jesus' name.

2. Every polygamy spirit in my life dies right now in Jesus' name.
3. I stand against every power of polygamy and destroy them by the fire of God Almighty.
4. I set my spouse free from the Incubus' spirits in Jesus' name.
5. I stand against every power of polygamy attacking my spouse, and destroying my physical marriage in Jesus' name.
6. Evil husband presently in my marriage causing confusion must receive the fire of God.
7. Evil wife presently in my marriage causing confusion must receive the fire of God.
8. Fire of God burns to ashes all foundation curses pursuing my marriage in Jesus' name.
9. Evil trap of destruction against my spouse by the spirits of Jezebel fail woefully in Jesus' name.
10. Household wickedness controlling my home your assignment is over; die in Jesus' name.
11. Evil animal representing the spirits of polygamy in my life die immediately in Jesus' name.
12. Evil root of sexual perversion that enflames passion in my body, come out with your entire root in Jesus' name.
13. Every form of evil property in my life receives the fire of God.
14. Every form of evil property in my spouse's life receives the fire of God.
15. Every form of evil property in my marriage receives fire of God.
16. All injuries in my marriage, the blood of Jesus Christ heals them now in Jesus' name.
17. Plantation of polygamy upon my marriage come out with your entire roots in Jesus' name.
18. Ancestral curse affecting my marriage through the spirits of polygamy die in Jesus' name.

19. Issues of polygamy dancing on my doorstep catch the fire of God in Jesus' name.

20. The power of Jesus nullifies all issues of polygamy in my life in Jesus' name.

21. Jehovah Lord destroys every polygamy habit running rampant in my marriage in Jesus' name.

22. I bind and paralyze you, spirit of polygamy, from my life in Jesus' name.

23. Foundational polygamy from my father's side running riot in my life catch the fire of God in Jesus' name.

24. Foundational polygamy from my mother's side running riot in my life catch the fire of God in Jesus' name.

25. Blood of Jesus Christ, purge me from every evil power of polygamy in Jesus' name.

26. Errors of divorce singing on my door waiting to enter catch the fire of God in Jesus' name.

27. Errors of divorce manipulating the mind of my spouse catch the fire of God in Jesus' name.

28. Heavenly Father, do not let my past record affect my life today in Jesus' name.

29. Every negative image of my past catches fire from God in Jesus' name.

30. Heavenly Father, give me a newness of life, and create in me a new heart full of the fear of the Lord in Jesus' name.

31. Christ, I invite You to live in my heart whether my enemies like it or not in Jesus' name.

32. Angels of the living God, hunt down every power of polygamy upon my marriage in Jesus' name.

33. Powers of the Lord chase down every power of polygamy upon my life in Jesus' name.

34. I shall never bow to any idol powers in Jesus' name.

35. I shall never dance to the tune of Satan the rest of my life in Jesus' name.

36. Every power preventing my marriage to continue be paralyzed in Jesus' name.

37. I bind and render as nothing all the power of all seducers attacking my marriage in Jesus' name.
38. Satanic birds eating up the love of my marriage die in Jesus' name.
39. I will not let my marriage dance to the tune of the devil in Jesus' name.
40. Heavenly Father, help me correct every mistake in my marriage in Jesus' name.
41. Anti-marriage powers linking to my ancestors fighting die in Jesus' name.
42. Wicked devices of the enemies upon my marriage be defeated in Jesus' name.
43. Spirits of polygamy your assignment is over; collide with the Rock of Ages in Jesus' name.
44. Good things in my life stolen by the spirit of polygamy be returned to me tenfold in Jesus' name.
45. Good things in my marriage taken by the spirits of household wickedness be returned tenfold in Jesus' name.
46. Father Lord, seize every activity of the spirits of household wickedness attacking my marriage in Jesus' name.
47. Father Lord, seize every activity of the spirits of household wickedness attacking my life in Jesus' name.
48. Father Lord, seize every activity of the spirits of household wickedness attacking my spouse's life in Jesus' name.
49. I shall never give up; the problems in my marriage shall give up in Jesus' name.
50. The problems in my marriage shall give up whether my enemies like it or not in Jesus' name.
51. The problems in my spouse's life shall give up by the power of the blood of Jesus Christ.
52. Powers of home wreckers looking to wreck my home, hear me now, my home is not your candidate in Jesus' name.
53. Spirit of home wrecker after my life, my life is not your candidate; die in Jesus' name.
54. Spirit of home wrecker after my spouse die in Jesus' name.

55. Spirit of polygamy, hear me and hear me well, my marriage is not your candidate in Jesus' name.
56. Spirit of polygamy attacking my marriage I sentence you to the Lake of Fire in Jesus' name.
57. Evil powers militating against my marriage be destroyed now in Jesus' name.
58. Lord Jesus, let the sword of fire pierce through the heart of the spirit of polygamy over my life in Jesus' name.
59. Father Lord, I thank You for delivering my marriage and me from the spirits of polygamy in Jesus' name.
60. Amen.

You must command the evil spirits to leave you.

You must continue to rebuke them *seven times* by the power of the blood of Jesus Christ, and they will leave you in Jesus' name.

You evil spirits that cause me to be bound to the attacks destroying my marriage, I destroy you and all your destroyers by the power of the blood of Jesus Christ. I renounce you and all your associate demons, and all your works in my life; I command you in the mighty name of Jesus Christ to lose your grip and release my marriage and me now by the thunder fire of God, in the matchless name of Jesus Christ I pray. Amen.

Chapter 19

Breaking Evil Marital Blood Covenants

You may be wondering what a blood covenant is. A blood covenant is a bond between life and death. A covenant is a contract or an agreement between two or more parties.

A covenant is serious, especially when signing a contract with devil. It is the form of agreement that is legally binding on the parties involved, meaning one cannot breach the contract — if you break the contract, you will die!

Why it is many people tend to enter into a blood covenant with anyone that they sleep with? They say things like:

I entered into a blood covenant with her because the first day I saw her, I knew she was the one God has prepared for me — especially the way she winks her eye at me, and my heart begins to pound. I knew she was the chosen one that God has prepared for me.

I entered into a blood covenant with him because he is filthy rich, and I always wanted a rich man in my life. I know for sure he was a God sent.

Oh, I entered into the blood covenant with her because I really like her big thighs.

I enter into a blood covenant with her because any time I see her, I tend to forget everything I'm supposed to do.

I enter into a blood covenant with her because her eyes make me crazy.

I entered into a blood covenant with her because her butt alone drives me nuts.

I enter into a blood covenant with her because she is rich, and I always wanted a rich woman in my life to support my lifestyle habits since I don't like to work.

I entered into a blood covenant with her because at my age, I always wanted a younger girl as my wife.

I entered into a blood covenant with him because I have a strong urge for younger men with muscles, and he really has all that I need from a man.

I entered into a blood covenant with him because I think he is cute.

I enter into a blood covenant with her because I think she is cute.

What are the consequences of such a covenant?

If you happen to have an evil blood covenant, they are in place until death tears us apart—the same as marriage vows: for better or for worse. Satanic agents that you enter into a covenant with are not going to let you go. Once you enter into the covenant, there is no turning back.

A covenant made in the physical world is as strong as the one made in the spirit realm, especially if it is made between human and unseen evil spirit. The consequences of such a covenant are horrible.

Some enter into covenants willingly, and there are some that make the covenant unwillingly. Making a covenant unwillingly happens through the forces of the evil spirits. Many individuals enter into an evil covenant through their parents, doings; others enter into an evil covenants, through inheritances from their parents or forefathers because of the idols they served.

There are others that make deliberate decision to enter a wrong covenant. They meet someone, and because of the way they look, they feel in love then decide to make a covenant with that individual. They may cut themselves in front of each other then each one will drink the other's blood swearing to each other, "I love you and I will never leave you as long as I live." Thus, they enter into a covenant by decision.

Parents can make covenants with demons for protection of their children. Once made, these evil covenants remain a hidden force that follows the family wherever they go ostensibly for protection, but actually for evil purposes. It is a demonic legacy.

There are many people today who suffer many problems in their lives, and a lot of the problems are caused by an evil, hidden covenant. These hidden-force covenants are strong and are the same as physical covenants, because many of the people covenanted with—not all of them—are human. Physically, they appear human, but spiritually, they are demons. Perhaps the one you enter into a covenant with physically may not be an agent of darkness, but the demons they serve are in the kingdom of darkness. Therefore, after making such a covenant with the physical person, his or her gods follow you wherever you go.

When most people who are not born again—just going to church once in a while does not make you born again—enter into a situation in their lives that seems to take forever for the issue to go away, sometimes it never goes away. The hidden covenants made by parents or grandparents cause problems without them knowing the implication of it or even knowing about the covenants—that's one reason why they are hidden.

Many evil forces use some people while they sleep. These people do not dream at all because powers of the night crippled them by wiping their memory while they sleep. Such people are tormented physically and emotionally because dreams serve a healthy, mental purpose. If they happen to have a dream, that dream is usually about having intercourse with a spirit wife or a spirit husband.

> Because you have said, "We have made a covenant with death, and with Sheol we have made a pact. The overwhelming scourge will not reach us when it passed by, for we have made falsehood our refuge and we have concealed ourselves with deception." – Isaiah 28:15

A solution to such issues is by deliverance or through prayer and reading the word of the Lord daily! The word of the Lord tells us that our covenant with death shall be canceled.

Your covenant with death will be canceled, and your pact with Sheol will not stand; when the overwhelming scourge passes through, then you become its trampling place. – Isaiah 28:18:

There is another kind of covenant made by God our creator. The mighty God we serve is a covenant-keeping God. Once you made a covenant with Him, He Jehovah will never break His covenant with you and He will always protect you from the hands of the wicked.

For the Lord your God is a compassionate God; He will not fail you nor destroy you nor forget the covenant with your fathers which He swore to them. – Deuteronomy 4:32

His word makes it impossible for Him to lie. He is a true, covenant keeping God.

I can testify to that. He is a provider, a giver…He actually makes impossible things possible if you trust and believe in Him. I did put my trust in Him, and to my surprise, He embarrassed me by proving me wrong. I shouldn't have been here, but by His mighty power He turned impossible things in my life into possible.

I really urge everyone that has made a covenant with Him to keep your covenant with Him.

What a mighty and covenant-keeping God we serve!

God is not a man, that He should lie, nor a son of man, that He should repent; has He said, and will He not do it? Or has He spoken, and will He not make it good? – Numbers 23:19

On the other hand, we have Satan that promises many people but never keeps any of his promises. He actually makes people's lives miserable. Covenants with him are death pacts.

Covenants made by our ancestors to their gods still travel in our generations. We may need to break some of these covenants, as most of them do not serve the one, true God.

Furthermore, I have heard the groaning of the sons of Israel, because the Egyptians are holding them in bondage, and I have remembered My covenant. – Exodus 6:5

There are covenants we make with the devil. There are covenants that were made by our forefathers without our knowledge, but are still traveling in our generation today. We must break all these evil, ungodly covenants in our lives, those made by deliberate choice by self, by family or by ancestor.

Every ungodly covenant made is a violation of the word of the Lord.

You shall make no covenant with them or with their gods – Exodus 23:32

Covenants made by our Lord Jesus Christ are the only covenants accepted and recognized by God our creator.

For this is My blood of the covenant, which is poured out for many for forgiveness of sins. – Matthew 26:28

You must ask for forgiveness to break these evil covenants in our lives. No matter if the covenant is not of your own making, sin – we have all sinned and come short of the glory of God – sin must be dealt with before God can do a cleansing work in your life. You must pray sincerely that the good Lord will break every evil covenants in your life and set you free from every demonic bondage that binds you.

Prayer

God Almighty, I am a sinner with unclean lips. Father Lord, have mercy upon me. Heavenly Father, I come unto Your presence for forgiveness. Any sin in my life that would hinder my prayer from being answered, Jehovah Lord, forgive me in Jesus' name. Anyone I have sinned against that I do not know about, Lord Jesus, forgive me in Jesus' name. Amen.

1. Everlasting Redeemer, I come into Your presence through the power of the blood of Jesus Christ. I submit my life unto You; take total control over every department in my life in

Jesus' name. Jehovah Lord, I ask that every sinful lifestyle and all immorality upon my life burn into ashes in Your thunder fire in Jesus' name.

2. Jehovah Lord, remove from my life completely all evil powers that are controlling my mind, soul, and body, in Jesus' name. I bind and paralyze every spirit in charge of any evil covenant in my life in Jesus' name.

3. Blood of Jesus Christ escort into the lake of fire all evil strangers in my life fueling any covenant made without my consent in Jesus' name.

4. I overthrow you spirit-enforcing, evil covenants in my life; release me now in Jesus' name.

5. Everything transferred into my life through demonic hands, lose your hold in Jesus' name.

6. Our God Our Father, I take the authority You gave me through Your Son and renounce all sins and iniquities from my life. Every covenant outside God's Kingdom that engages me, Lord Jesus, break and destroy them in Jesus' name.

7. I flush out by the power of the blood of Jesus Christ all demonic consumptions transferred into my life.

8. Jehovah Lord, let Your thunder fire destroy every spirit of death and Hell against my life in Jesus' name.

9. Heavenly Father, let Your thunder fire destroy every spirit of death and Hell upon my family in Jesus' name.

10. Covenants of my ancestors following my generation today, I break your powers over my life in Jesus' name.

11. Covenant from my father's side harassing my life your power hold is broken in my life, broken and destroyed in Jesus' name.

12. Covenant in my mother's side controlling my life and my marriage I break and cancel your power out of my life and my marriage by the power of the blood of Jesus Christ.

13. Fire of God, destroy all demonic soul ties instituted by my ancestors that follow me around; let Your fire escort them

side by side to the Lake of Fire and destroy them in Jesus' name.

14. Stubborn demons from my forefathers still operating and running riot in my family your spiritual assignment upon my life is over; perish now in Jesus' name.

15. Father Lord, let the yoke of my ancestors be broken into pieces in Jesus.

16. Blood of Jesus Christ destroy every evil garment I am spiritually wearing made by my ancestors in Jesus' name.

17. I bind and cast out every associate demon fueling problems in my life in Jesus' name.

18. All foundational poverty running in my family dies in Jesus' name.

19. Evil stranger protecting my home, the fire of God destroys them all in Jesus' name.

20. Spirit of the living God, arise in your power, and destroy all financial devourers working on my family in Jesus' name.

21. I break every curse of failure operating in my life and family in Jesus' name.

22. Every covenant with water spirits upon my life and family break in Jesus' name.

23. Every covenant with desert spirits upon my life and family break in Jesus' name.

24. Every covenant with family gods upon my life and family break in Jesus' name.

25. Every covenant with evil, family guardian spirits in my life and family break in Jesus' name.

26. All covenants with witchcraft spirits in my life and family break in Jesus' name.

27. Every covenant with masquerade spirits in my life and family, break in Jesus' name.

28. Every covenant with an inherited spirit husband in my life break in Jesus' name.

29. Every covenant with an inherited spirit wife in my life break in Jesus' name.

30. Curses of automatic failure from my ancestors in my life and marriage, your legal hold is broken now by the power of the blood of Jesus Christ.
31. Evil plantation of failure growing in my family line is uprooted and destroyed now in Jesus' name.
32. Evil soul-tie covenant made with my ancestors break by the power of the blood of Jesus Christ.
33. Every soul-tie covenant made with my grandfather break by the power of the blood of Jesus Christ.
34. Every soul-tie covenant made with my grandmother break by the power of the blood of Jesus Christ.
35. Every soul-tie covenant made with my ex-girlfriend's ancestors that have legal hold on me break now by the power of the blood of Jesus Christ.
36. Every soul-tie covenant with my ex-boyfriend's ancestors that have legal hold on me break now by the power of the blood of Jesus Christ.
37. Let the wicked spirit vows spoken over my life be broken now in Jesus' name.
38. I seize the power from every legion operating in my life in Jesus' name.
39. All spiritual warfare attacking my providence die in Jesus' name.
40. Evil forces bargaining for my providence backfire by fire in Jesus' name.
41. Spirit of mistakes and errors assigned against my providence die in Jesus' name.
42. Evil vows made by my ancestors, contrary to my providence break now in Jesus' name.
43. Every evil vow made by my forefathers affecting my marriage break now by the power of the blood of Jesus Christ.
44. Every evil vow made by my spouse's forefathers affecting my marriage break now by the power of the blood of Jesus Christ.

45. Every ancestral, evil guardian spirit in my life be destroyed by the power of the blood of Jesus Christ.

46. Every parental guardian spirit in my life be destroyed by the power of the blood of Jesus Christ.

47. Every curse placed on my ancestors by anybody through sexual perversion that now affects my generation the power of the blood of Jesus Christ breaks you now.

48. Every curse placed on my ancestors by anybody through prostitution affecting my generation breaks now by the power of the blood of Jesus Christ.

49. Every curse placed on my ancestors by anybody through bestiality spirits affecting my generation breaks now by the power of the blood of Jesus Christ.

50. Every curse placed on my ancestors by anybody through Zoophilia spirits affecting my generation breaks now by the power of the blood of Jesus Christ.

51. Every curse placed on my ancestors by anybody through spirits of gender manipulation affecting my generation breaks now by the power of the blood of Jesus Christ.

52. Every curse placed on my ancestors by anybody through spirits of cheating affecting my generation breaks now by the power of the blood of Jesus Christ.

53. Every curse placed on my ancestors affecting my generation by anybody inadvertently breaks now by the power of the blood of Jesus Christ.

54. Every curse of infirmities, sicknesses, or diseases passed down to my generation catch the fire from God in Jesus' name.

55. Every curse of incurable disease passed down to my generation catch the fire from God in Jesus' name.

56. Every curse of barrenness passed down to my generation catch the fire from God in Jesus' name.

57. Every curse of poverty passed down to my generation catch the fire from God in Jesus' name.

58. Every curse of frustration passed down to my generation catch the fire from God in Jesus' name.
59. Every curse of depression passed down to my generation catch the fire from God in Jesus' name.
60. Every curse of sadness passed down to my generation catch the fire from God in Jesus' name.
61. Every curse of anger and bitterness passed down to my generation catch the fire from God in Jesus' name.
62. Every evil, ancestral river flowing down my generation be sealed now by the power of the blood of Jesus Christ.
63. Every weakness of moral failure manifesting in my life lose your hold of me in Jesus' name.
64. Powers of my father's side seeking to make a shipwreck of my life be destroyed by the fire of God.
65. Powers of my mother's side seeking to make a shipwreck of my life be destroyed by the fire of God.
66. Father Lord, I thank You for delivering me from the hands of the spirits of evil marital blood covenants in Jesus' name.
67. Amen.

You must command the evil spirits to leave you.

You must continue to rebuke them *seven times* by the power of the blood of Jesus Christ, and they will leave you in Jesus' name.

You evil spirits binding me by the attacks of evil, blood covenants, I destroy you and all of your blood covenants over my life by the power of the blood of Jesus Christ. I renounce you, and all your associate demons, and all your works in my life. I break myself loose and cancel every covenant with you and every associate demon such as spirit of perversion, spirit of gender manipulation, spirit of pornography, spirit of bestiality, and spirit of Zoophilia. I command you in the mighty name of Jesus Christ to lose your grip and release my marriage and me now by the thunder fire of God, in the matchless name of Jesus Christ I pray. Amen.

Chapter 20

Destroying Marital Yokes

There are many people that have strange, ungodly histories in their families. Most already have a curse that earlier generations placed upon their families. There are also families where there are very strong, evil covenants that protect such families; therefore, if one marries into such a family, the curse will follow your marriage filling it with one after the other problems.

> From the days of John the Baptist until now the kingdom of Heaven suffers violence and violent men take it by force.
>
> – Matthew 11:12:
>
> He delivers me from my enemies; surely, You lift me above those who rise up against me; you rescue me from the violent man. – Psalm 18:48:

Prayer

1. Lord Jesus, render impotent the imagination of the enemy upon my marriage in Jesus' name.
2. I bind and cast into the pit every anti-marriage spell and curse upon my marriage in Jesus' name.
3. I destroy every bewitchment fashioned against my marriage in Jesus' name.
4. I destroy every evil covenant of marital failure fashioned against my marriage by the power of the blood of Jesus Christ.
5. Blood of Jesus Christ, destroy every evil wedding made by Satan in the spirit realm in Jesus' name.
6. I neutralize every incision placed in my body as a mark by a spirit wife or a spirit husband in Jesus' name.

7. Every sign of anti-marriage marked into my life is destroyed in Jesus' name.

8. Father Lord, wherever Satan has placed my providence, restore them in their original position in Jesus' name.

9. I stand against the Spirit of Destruction that challenges my marriage in Jesus' name.

10. Every spirit bargaining for my marriage dies in Jesus' name.

11. Weapons of strongman used against my marriage collide with the Rock of Ages in Jesus' name.

12. Blood of Jesus Christ, wipe clean any past record that the enemy is using against my marriage in Jesus' name.

13. I break lose every bondage of marital confusion harassing my marriage in Jesus' name.

14. Let God arise, and let my enemies scatter in Jesus' name.

15. Father Lord scatters every enemy of my marriage in Jesus' name.

16. Father Lord destroys frustration and disappointments aggravating my marriage in Jesus' name.

17. I bind and paralyze every power of setback ruining the restoration of my marriage in Jesus' name.

18. Powers of the night draining my virtue die in Jesus' name.

19. Evil powers of stagnation over my marriage die in Jesus' name.

20. God, arise and scatter every enemy that has refused to let me go in Jesus' name.

21. God, arise and scatter every enemy that has refused to let my marriage go in Jesus' name.

22. Father Lord, lead my stubborn pursuers into the Lake of Fire in Jesus' name.

23. Lord Jesus, send Your axe of fire into the root of all evil plantations upon my marriage and destroy them in Jesus' name.

24. Every satanic seed upon my marriage, be uprooted in Jesus' name.

25. I break every evil covenant from the day I was born till now in Jesus' name.

26. God of a new beginning, start a new thing in my life in Jesus' name.

27. God of a new beginning, begin a new thing in my marriage in Jesus' name.

28. Holy Ghost fire, fall upon my marriage in Jesus' name.

29. Holy Ghost, the holy fire of God, burn everything in my body, soul and spirit that is evil in Jesus' name.

30. Holy Ghost fire, burn everything of no God in my marriage in Jesus' name.

31. Any ungodly image representing my marriage in the demonic world perishes now in Jesus' name.

32. Father Lord, I withdraw my marriage from the hands of the strongman in Jesus' name.

33. I cancel and break every evil vow by my ancestors on my behalf in Jesus' name.

34. Every evil barrier between my spouse and me, be canceled now in Jesus' name.

35. I bind and cancel every Spirit of Loneliness bargaining for my life in Jesus' name.

36. I bind and cancel every Spirit of Lateness in my life in Jesus' name.

37. I bind and cancel every Spirit of Sadness bargaining for my life in Jesus' name.

38. I bind and cancel every Spirit of Death and Hell bargaining for my life in Jesus' name.

39. I bind and cancel every witchcraft activity upon my life in Jesus' name.

40. I bind and cancel every sorcerer's activity upon my life in Jesus' name.

41. I bind and cancel every dream marriage in my life in Jesus' name.

42. I bind and cancel every Spirit of Sexual Perversion upon my life in Jesus' name.

43. I bind and cancel every marital yoke upon my life in Jesus' name.
44. I bind and cancel every evil mask upon my face in Jesus' name.
45. Every seed of the oppression upon my marriage, die in Jesus' name.
46. Every yoke of oppression upon my marriage, break in Jesus' name.
47. Spiritual bullets fired against my marriage, collide with the rock of ages in Jesus' name.
48. No evil shall befall my marriage; my spouse and I shall continue our marriage whether our enemies like it or not in Jesus' name.
49. Powers of diversion and seduction, release my marriage in Jesus' name.
50. Every yoke of stagnancy challenging my marriage, break in Jesus' name.
51. Demonic powers fighting to break my marriage, die in Jesus' name.
52. Satanic powers of failure bargaining for my marriage, perish now in Jesus' name.
53. Any evil power that has vowed to destroy my marriage, die now in Jesus' name.
54. Yoke of foundational curse after my marriage, your time is up; die now in Jesus' name.
55. Satanic cage to which my spouse and I have been tied down, catch the fire of God now in Jesus' name.
56. Every root of hardship challenging my marriage, fight yourself to the death in Jesus' name.
57. Fire of God destroys every item in my house that has been representing the demonic world in Jesus' name.
58. My spouse and I shall never bow to any demonic idols in Jesus' name.
59. My marriage, anchor to the voice of the Lord in Jesus' name.

60. Father Lord, I thank You for delivering my marriage from every demonic attack in Jesus' name.
61. Amen.

You must command the evil spirits to leave you.

You must continue to rebuke them *seven times* by the power of the blood of Jesus Christ, and they will leave you in Jesus' name.

You evil spirits that cause me to be bound to the attacks of marital yokes, I destroy you and all of your destroyers over my marriage, by the power of the blood of Jesus Christ. I renounce you and all your associate demons, and all your works in my life; I command you in the mighty name of Jesus Christ to lose your grip and release my marriage and me now by the thunder fire of God, in the matchless name of Jesus Christ I pray. Amen.

Chapter 21

Setting Children Free from Satanic Bondage

Many parents tend to forget their children while battling to resolve marital issues. If there are heated marital issues going on at home while children are present, most of the time the evils intend to possess the children and use the children to start causing all sorts of confusion all over again. It is always advisable for the parents to pray with their children during the whole process.

> *Thus says the Lord who made you and formed you from the womb, who will help you, "Do not fear, O Jacob My servant; and you, Jeshurun, whom I have chosen." – Isaiah 44:2:*

Prayer

Father Lord, I come against many evil attacks upon my children's lives in Jesus' name. Destroy Powers of the night fighting for my children without recognition in Jesus' name. Jehovah Lord, take charge, take absolute control over my children's lives, deliver them from the hands of the wicked in Jesus' name. Amen.

1. I rise against any power bargaining for my children in Jesus' name.
2. I deliver my children from the hands of the wicked in Jesus' name.
3. I bind and destroy the spirit of fear in my children's lives in Jesus' name.
4. I destroy any demons inside my children's room in Jesus' name.
5. Evil powers that prefer hiding in the children's room the fire of God destroys them in Jesus' name.
6. Heavenly Father, fill my children with the Holy Spirit in Jesus' name.

7. I bind every ancestral spirit in my children's lives in Jesus' name.
8. I bind every demonic spirit in my children's lives in Jesus' name.
9. I bind every witchcraft power in my children's lives in Jesus' name.
10. I break every parental curse in my children's lives in Jesus' name.
11. I bind and paralyze every evil spirit controlling my children's lives in Jesus' name.
12. I bind and paralyze every spirit of rage controlling my children's lives in Jesus' name.
13. I bind and paralyze every spirit of anger controlling my children's lives in Jesus' name.
14. I bind and paralyze every spirit of bitterness attacking my children's lives in Jesus' name.
15. I bind and paralyze every spirit of fighting in my children's lives in Jesus' name.
16. I bind and paralyze every spirit of rebellion in my children's lives in Jesus' name.
17. I bind and paralyze every spirit of confusion in my children's lives in Jesus' name.
18. I bind and paralyze every spirit of depression in my children's lives in Jesus' name.
19. I bind and paralyze every spirit of sorrow in my children's lives in Jesus' name.
20. I bind and paralyze every spirit of madness in my children's lives in Jesus' name.
21. I bind and paralyze every spirit of foul mouth in my children's mouth in Jesus' name.
22. I bind and paralyze spirits of drugs in my children's lives in Jesus' name.
23. I bind and paralyze spirit of alcohol in my children's lives in Jesus' name.

24. I bind and paralyze every spirit of bullying in my children's lives in Jesus' name.
25. I bind and paralyze every spirit of abuse in my children's lives in Jesus' name.
26. I set my children free from the hands of the wicked in Jesus' name.
27. I decree total blessings of God over every department in my children's lives in Jesus' name.
28. I plead the blood of Jesus Christ upon my children's lives in Jesus' name.
29. I shield my children under the rock of Christ Jesus.
30. I decree favor upon my children in Jesus' name.
31. I decree joy upon my children's lives in Jesus' name.
32. I decree peace upon my children's lives in Jesus' name.
33. I speak deliverance of fervency upon my children's lives in Jesus' name.
34. I release the fire of God upon my children's lives in Jesus' name.
35. Jesus Christ, live inside my children's lives in Jesus' name.
36. I decree all promises of God shall manifest upon my children in Jesus' name.
37. Signs and wonders of God overflow upon my children in Jesus' name.
38. Disgrace shall never come upon my children in Jesus' name.
39. Shame shall never be the portion of my children in Jesus' name.
40. Embarrassment shall never be a portion of my children's lives in Jesus' name.
41. Disappointment shall never be a portion of my children's lives in Jesus' name.
42. Affliction shall never come upon my children's lives in Jesus' name.
43. God, conquer and save my children's lives.
44. I decree and declare that no generational curse shall befall my children in Jesus' name.

45. I decree and declare that no ancestral curse shall befall my children in Jesus' name.
46. Fire of God encircles my children's lives day and night in Jesus' name.
47. Holy Ghost fire take absolute control upon my children's lives in Jesus' name.
48. My children shall not die before their time in Jesus' name.
49. Everlasting Father, I thank You for delivering my children from the satanic bondage in Jesus' name.
50. Amen.

You must command the evil spirits to leave you.

You must continue to rebuke them *seven times* by the power of the blood of Jesus Christ, and they will leave you in Jesus' name.

You evil spirits that cause children to be bound to satanic bondage, I renounce you and all your associate demons, and all your works in my children's lives; I command you in the mighty name of Jesus Christ to lose your grip and release my marriage and me now by the thunder fire of God, in the matchless name of Jesus Christ I pray. Amen.

Deliverance from the Marriage Breakers

Chapter 22

Every believer tormented by the spirits of marriage breaker should pray these prayers to have your marriage restored in Jesus' name. These spirits of marriage breaker are patient and clever spirits that intend to stay with couples for years until they finally get finished achieving their assignment of marriage breakup. If you are the target victim, and the spirits noticed your prayer life is too violent for them to enter you marriage, they stay distant but keep following you until they find a chink in your armor. They get their hands on you by destroying your marriage.

Once you are the target, if they don't succeed in their assignment to destroy your marriage, and if they return empty-handed to the kingdom of darkness, these evil spirits will be tortured. Therefore, they will make sure they accomplish their assignment before they return to give their report. They cannot stand homes that are filled with prayers daily. I urge everyone, no matter what your situation may be, either good or bad, do not cease praying as the devil is out to kill and destroy homes and marriages.

> *The thief comes only to steal and kill and destroy; I came that they may have life, and have it abundantly.* – John 10:10
>
> *For this reason, a man shall leave his father and mother. And the two shall become one flesh; so they are no longer two, but one flesh. What therefore God has joined together let no man separate.* – Mark 10:7-9

Prayer

In Jesus' name, in the powerful name of Jesus Christ, the great I Am that I am, Thou ever faithful God, we praise Your Holy name. We magnify Your name. We thank You for Your deliverance and setting us free from the hands of the spirits of marriage breakers in Jesus' name.

1. I destroy every yoke of satanic spell over my marriage in Jesus' name.
2. Father Lord, establish my marriage on the rock in Jesus' name.
3. I cancel every evil marital contract over my marriage in Jesus' name.
4. Heavenly Father, let all spirits of marriage breakers be torn from my marriage in Jesus' name.
5. I bind and paralyze every spirit of broken home out of my home in Jesus' name.
6. I bind and paralyze every spirit of familiar spirit out of my home in Jesus' name.
7. I bind and paralyze every spirit of lying out of my home and life in Jesus' name.
8. I bind and paralyze every spirit of fornication out of my home and life in Jesus' name.
9. I bind and paralyze every spirit of adultery out of my home and life in Jesus' name.
10. I bind and paralyze every spirit of Jezebel out of my home and life in Jesus' name.
11. I bind and paralyze every spirit of lust out of my home and life in Jesus' name.
12. I break every satanic cage trapping my marriage in Jesus' name.
13. Evil seducers seducing my marriage die in Jesus' name.
14. Marriage breakers on assignment to destroy my marriage die in Jesus' name.
15. Marriage breakers bargaining for my marriage die in Jesus' name.
16. Father Lord, turn every curse upon my marriage into blessings in Jesus' name.
17. I deliver my marriage from the hands of the home wreckers in Jesus' name.
18. Powers of marriage killers on assignment to kill my marriage backfire by fire.

19. I break the backbone of marriage breakers in Jesus' name.
20. I break the backbone of marriage destroyers in Jesus' name.
21. I break the backbone of marriage discomfort in Jesus' name.
22. I break the backbone of marriage frustrations in Jesus' name.
23. I break the backbones of spirits of fornication in Jesus' name.
24. I break the backbone of the spirit of prostitution in Jesus' name.
25. I break the backbones of spirits of broken marriage and harassment in Jesus' name.
26. Storms of confusion depart from my marriage in Jesus' name.
27. God, arise with Your weapon and lead the evil strangers upon my marriage into the Lake of Fire in Jesus' name.
28. Powers of the night pursuing my marriage die in Jesus' name.
29. Evil powers working on restructuring my marriage backfire by fire in Jesus' name.
30. Fire of God burns every evil foundation within my marriage in Jesus' name.
31. Spirits of poverty and confusion challenging my marriage die in Jesus' name.
32. Strange gods attacking my marriage perish now in Jesus' name.
33. Every enemy performing devastating strategies against my marriage collide with the Rock of Ages in Jesus' name.
34. Every habitation of cruelty fashioned against my marriage become desolate in Jesus' name.
35. I erase and destroy completely every past record of evil intent upon my marriage in Jesus' name.
36. Lord, perfect Your good work upon my marriage.

37. Jehovah Lord, perfect what is lacking in my marriage in Jesus' name.
38. Holy Ghost fire arrest the spirits of marriage breaker in every department in my marriage in Jesus' name.
39. Evil doors that are open in my marriage be sealed by the power of the blood of Jesus Christ.
40. Father Lord, I thank You for delivering my marriage from the hands of the marriage breakers in Jesus' name.
41. Amen.

You must command the evil spirits to leave you.

You must continue to rebuke them *seven times* by the power of the blood of Jesus Christ, and they will leave you in Jesus' name.

You evil spirits that cause me to be bound to the attacks of Marriage Breakers, I renounce you and all your associate demons, and all your works in my life. I command you in the mighty name of Jesus Christ to lose your grip and release my marriage and me now by the thunder fire of God, in the matchless name of Jesus Christ I pray. Amen.

Chapter 23

Friends Destroying Marriages

Too often, I hear those I counsel complain about their friends interfering in their marriage affairs. They will ask me questions like:

"Why it is that my friend always tries to interfere with my marriage affairs?"

"Is there a reason why my best friend always says something negative about my marriage?"

"If my friend always has something negative to say about my marriage, does that mean I should stop talking to them?"

One must learn how to keep private marital issues from friends since friends may be jealous of what you have. You go to your friends with your marital problems telling them all about the fight you had, or your feelings about what your spouse did the other night. That gives your friends the opportunity to talk negative about your marriage.

No, you shouldn't stop talking to your friends, but there is no need to talk to them about your private marriage affairs. If there is an issue in your marriage, you must find a professional counselor, or a minister with whom you discuss your marital problems – not your best friend.

"If my friend always engages me in activities that keep me away from my spouse, does that mean they want to destroy my marriage?"

If you continue following them, of course it will lead into destruction of your marriage.

Almost every day, my friend has complained about my spouse. Does it mean I should stop talking to them?

For the sake of peace, you should find a healthier friend than the one who is trying to stir up contentions between you and your spouse. What good comes from that?

If my best friend is always talking negative about my spouse, does it mean they are jealous of my marriage?

If they keep complaining about your spouse, it means they are jealous of you, and they are on assignment to destroy your marriage.

"I really love my best friend; I've known him/her since childhood. But he/she always has something negative to say about my relationship. Is that a threat to my marriage?"

You should engage your spouse with godly things, and if your best friend still has complaints about that, I advise you to look for new friends.

"I share every secret of mine with my best friend; is that something that can ruin my marriage?"

Yes, it can definitely destroy your marriage when your friend is not trustworthy. Sharing secrets with your friend instead of your spouse leads to your spouse's distrust of you. Too often people expend energy on friends that they should be spending on strengthening their marriage.

"There are things about me that only my best friend knows, and my spouse has no clue of it. Is that bad for my marriage?"

It's okay for your best friend to know some of your secrets; not all best friends are out to destroy your marriage. There are good Christian and non-Christian best friends who will encourage you to build your marriage. There are also friends that have an evil intent. They are green with envy, and all they think about is how to destroy your marriage. They will eat, drink, and laugh with us, and know the ins and outs of everything we do pretending they are on our side, but in reality, they are against everything we do.

I pray that the God of Abraham, Isaac, and Jacob, reveals these evil intents and purposes of so-called friends, and exposes them openly to you in Jesus' name.

Behold, I am laying in Zion a stone, a tested stone, a costly cornerstone for the foundation, firmly placed. He who believes in it will not be disturbed. – Isaiah 28:16

If anyone is destined for captivity, to captivity he goes; if anyone kills with the sword, with the sword he must be killed. Here is the perseverance and the faith of the saints.

– Revelation 13:10

The thief comes only to steal and kill and destroy; I came that they may have life, and have it abundantly. – John 10:10

Prayer

1. Woe to you, Oh destroyer, while you were not destroyed; and he who is treacherous, while others did not deal treacherously with him. As soon as you finish destroying, you will be destroyed; as soon as you cease to deal treacherously, others will deal treacherously with you.
2. I bind and cast out every evil friend in my life in Jesus' name.
3. Evil friends bargaining for my marriage catch the fire of God in Jesus' name.
4. Heavenly Father, let every yoke of a devourer against my marriage destroy its owner in Jesus' name.
5. Everlasting Redeemer, expose evil friends working secretly to destroy my marriage in Jesus' name.
6. Spirit of the living God, arise in Your power, and arrest every evil friend in my life that is against my marriage in Jesus' name.
7. Heavenly Father, curse a substitution against evil friends over my marriage to bow to the word of the Lord in Jesus' name.
8. God Almighty, dispatch Your angels to roll away every stumbling block in my marriage in Jesus' name.
9. Blood of Jesus escort affliction and hindrance upon my marriage to the pit of fire in Jesus' name.

10. Jehovah Lord against evil powers that are using my friends against my marriage let Your thunder fire strike the source of the problems in Jesus' name.

11. Powers of the night controlling issues in my marriage catch the fire of God in Jesus' name.

12. God Almighty, consume all evil strangers in my marriage in Jesus' name.

13. Holy Ghost fire burn up every yoke of marital afflictions in my life in Jesus' name.

14. I withdraw my marriage from the hands of the evil designers in Jesus' precious name.

15. I cancel and break every yoke of confusion and disagreement in my marriage in Jesus' name.

16. I break every grip of witchcraft activity over my marriage in Jesus' name.

17. I render every Goliath defying my marriage to bow to the word of the Lord.

18. Opposition of household wickedness using friends against my marriage catches the fire of God.

19. I refuse to reap evil harvest in my marriage in Jesus' name.

20. I plead the blood of Jesus Christ over my marriage in Jesus' name.

21. Power of God destroys every garment of reproach in my marriage in Jesus' name.

22. Angels of the living God, take charge, take control over all the evil friends against my marriage in Jesus' name.

23. Everlasting Father, I thank You for delivering my marriage from the hands of the evil friends in Jesus' name.

24. Amen.

You must command the evil spirits to leave you.

You must continue to rebuke them *seven times* by the power of the blood of Jesus Christ, and they will leave you in Jesus' name.

You evil spirits that cause me to be bound to the evil friends, I destroy you and all of your works over my marriage, by the power of the blood of Jesus Christ. I renounce you and all your associate demons, and all your works in my life; I command you in the mighty name of Jesus Christ to lose your grip and release my marriage and me now by the thunder fire of God, in the matchless name of Jesus Christ I pray. Amen.

Chapter 24

Hidden Curses on Your Marriage

Curses can follow families continually down through many generations. When a person has been cursed, an evil wish has been uttered against them that can cause spiritual and physical injury to come upon that person. These spells of witchcraft torment their family, and can affect later generations, by calamity, financial failure, infirmities, barrenness, frustration, anger, bitterness, disappointments, stagnancy, failure in everything they try to achieve, prostitution, bestiality, polygamy, sexual perversion, gender misunderstanding, and pornographic activities.

If you have been a victim of this nature, the solution to your problem is deliverance through spiritual warfare prayer. If you noticed any of these issues in your life, follow these prayer instructions and let God be God in your life.

> The word of the Lord and a prayer is the only solution to such situation. The Bible tells us that cursed is everyone who hangs on a tree. Like a sparrow in its flitting, like a swallow in its flying, so a curse without cause does not alight. – Proverbs 26:2
>
> Christ redeemed us from the curse of the Law, having become a curse for us for it is written, cursed is everyone who hangs on a tree. – Galatians 3:13

Prayer

Everlasting Father, I bless Your Holy name. Jehovah Lord, I magnify Your name.

Abba Father, I just want to thank You for You are the omnipresent God — the God of Isaac, God Jacob, and God of Abraham. I am here, this moment, to present my petition to You.

Heavenly Father, I confess to You that I have been under the bondage of (mention all the curses you been through in your life; for example: spirit of fornication, spirit of pornography, spirit of gender confusion, spirit of masturbation, spirit of murder, spirit of eaters of the flesh, spirit of financial failure, spirit of stagnancy, spirit of infirmities) and I ask, Lord Jesus, that You break each and every curse by the power of the blood of Jesus Christ.

Jehovah, Abba Father, I ask that You take charge of every situation in my life. I ask that You, Jehovah Lord, take total control of every curse placed upon my life, upon my family, upon my generation, that You break such evil spells and turn every evil in my life into total blessings. In Jesus' name I pray. Amen.

1. Heavenly Father, I am a sinner, I ask for forgiveness; Lord Jesus, any sin in my life that would hinder my prayer of being answered. Heavenly Father forgives me in Jesus' name.
2. I confess to You, Lord, that I've been under a satanic bondage and I ask that You break such curse upon my life by the power of the blood of Jesus Christ.
3. I break every ungodly tie that still binds my family and me in Jesus' name.
4. I renounce every contact with the occult and witchcraft activities, and call for the power of Jesus to destroy them completely in Jesus' name.
5. Every curse placed upon my life and family, be broken now in Jesus' name.
6. Spirit of Polygamy harassing my life, die in Jesus' name.
7. Spirit of polygamy running riot in my generation, catch the fire of God in Jesus' name.

8. I renounce all unholy covenants that my ancestors that are affecting my family and me to be broken by the matchless name of Jesus Christ.

9. The power of the Holy Ghost shall destroy every foundational witchcraft activity in my family line in Jesus' name.

10. Heavenly Father, let the power of the Holy Ghost destroy every foundational familiar spirit in my family in Jesus' name.

11. Father Lord, let the power of the Holy Ghost destroy every foundational water spirit activities in my family line in Jesus' name.

12. Jehovah Lord, let the power of the Holy Ghost destroy every spirit of calamity in my life, marriage, and family in Jesus' name.

13. Everlasting Redeemer, let the power of the Holy Ghost destroy every Spirit of Polygamy upon my life, marriage, and family in Jesus' name.

14. Jehovah Nissi, let the power of the Holy Ghost destroy every Spirit of Pornography attached to my life, marriage, and family in Jesus' name.

15. God Almighty, let the habitation of hidden curses over my life be desolate in Jesus' name.

16. Heavenly Father, let every stronghold of hidden curses upon my life be destroyed by the thunder fire of God.

17. Father, let the fire of the Holy Ghost burn up the diviners of hidden curses and make them impotent in Jesus' name.

18. Jehovah Lord, let the weapons of the hidden curses turn against them in Jesus' name.

19. Every spirit of bestiality over my life, break by fire of God.

20. Every spirit of pornography in my life break by fire of God.

21. Every spirit of prostitution in my life, break by fire of God.

22. Every spirit of gender manipulations in my life, break by fire of God.

23. Every spirit of gender confusion in my life, break by fire of God.
24. Every spirit of witchcraft activity in my life, break by fire of God.
25. Every spirit of barrenness upon my life, break by fire of God.
26. Every spirit of financial failure in my life, break by fire of God.
27. Every spirit of infirmity in my life, break by fire of God.
28. Every spirit of stagnancy in my life, break by fire of God.
29. Every spirit of frustration in my life, break by fire of God.
30. Every spirit of anger and bitterness in my life, break by fire of God.
31. Every spirit of theft in my life, break by fire of God.
32. Every devouring spirit upon my life, break by fire of God.
33. Every spirit of disgrace in my life, break by fire of God.
34. Every spirit of embarrassment in my life, break by fire of God.
35. Every demonic curse upon my life, break by fire of God.
36. I reverse every evil curse against my foundation in Jesus' name.
37. I deliver my soul from the hands of the wicked in Jesus' name.
38. I deliver my destiny from the hands of the strongman in Jesus' name.
39. Blood of Jesus, destroy every spirit of lateness fashion against my marriage in Jesus' name.
40. Blood of Jesus, break every spell and enchantment programmed against me in Jesus' name.
41. Blood of Jesus, destroy every spirit marriage in my life in Jesus' name.
42. Blood of Jesus, cancel every evil vow upon my life in Jesus' name.
43. I break and release myself from every evil, marital curse in Jesus' name.

44. Father Lord, let every family idol from both sides of my parents release my marriage and me by the power of the blood of Jesus Christ.
45. I revoke every spirit child in my life in Jesus' name.
46. I revoke every spirit husband in my life in Jesus' name.
47. I revoke every spirit wife in my life in Jesus' name.
48. I renounce all contacts with every occult practice I've been engaged in Jesus' name.
49. I renounce every sexual sin that the devil had introduced into my life in Jesus' name.
50. I renounce all unholy covenants my forefathers have made upon my generation in Jesus' name.
51. I divorce myself completely from the spirit of pride in Jesus' name.
52. I renounce all curses that I have brought upon myself whether knowingly or unknowingly, through witchcraft and occult practices, by the power of the blood of Jesus Christ.
53. Lord Jesus, let every territorial woman and the strongmen bargaining for my marriage bow to the word of the Lord.
54. Every demonic power involved in the evil attacks upon my life, cease your activities in my life, my family, and my marriage by the thunder fire of God.
55. Father Lord breaks every evil vow in my life and turns all tears into laughter in Jesus' name.
56. Lord Jesus turns every disappointment in my life into divine appointments in Jesus' name.
57. Jehovah Lord replaces all marital curses and covenants upon my life into divine blessings in Jesus' name.
58. I shield my life, my family, my marriage, and my finances in the blood of Jesus Christ.
59. Jehovah Lord, I thank You for answering my prayer in Jesus' name. Amen.

You must command the evil spirits to leave you.

You must continue to rebuke them *seven times* by the power of the blood of Jesus Christ, and they will leave you in Jesus' name.

You evil spirits that cause me to be bound to the attacks of hidden curses upon my marriage, I destroy you and all of your destroyers over my marriage by the power of the blood of Jesus Christ, I renounce you and all your associate demons, and all your works in my life. I command you in the mighty name of Jesus Christ to lose your grip and release my marriage and me now by the thunder fire of God, in the matchless name of Jesus Christ I pray. Amen.

Chapter 25

Destroying Barrenness

The devil has made many childless, or perhaps a better term is fruitless.

Barrenness is not limited to child bearing. Barrenness is a lack of results, or no achievements. It applies to marriage, health, business, missions, and finances.

Everything that does not produce results, we call barren. That state is against God's will for your life. As we are all descendants of Abraham, everything we touch must prosper and be productive through God's will for mankind.

Jehovah Lord has given us the power to be fruitful in every department in our lives. Satan and his agents have no power to stop us in Jesus' name.

There shall be no one miscarrying or barren in your land; I will fulfill the number of your days. – Exodus 23:26

There are many people that start new projects but never finish them. The spirits of almost-there cripples those people. Barrenness and poverty have taken a toll on their businesses, so consequently, when they are supposed to win, they lose. I prophesy that whether your enemies like it or not, you will possess your possessions today in Jesus' name.

> But on Mount Zion, there will be those who escape, and it will
> be holy. And the house of Jacob will possess their possessions.
>
> – Obadiah 1:17

Prayer

Jehovah Lord, I come to You in the name of Jesus Christ. I claim the promises of God about childbearing over my life in Jesus' name. Father Lord, You said by Your stripes we shall be healed. Heavenly Father, I am in agreement with Your word. I ask that You heal my womb from every problem of barrenness in Jesus' name. Father Lord, destroy every form of barrenness in my life in Jesus' name. I bind and paralyze everything that is hindering me from conceiving and birthing in Jesus' name. I receive my pregnancy breakthrough today by the power of the blood of Jesus Christ. Amen.

1. By power of the blood of Jesus Christ, I prophesy upon my life that every satanic hindrance upon my life must be broken now in Jesus' name.

2. I decree that that I shall be productive from my barrenness in Jesus' name.

3. I decree that I shall bear a child by the power of the blood of Jesus Christ.

4. I decree that the God of Isaac, Jacob, and Abraham shall be my provider in my marriage in Jesus' name.

5. I decree that every hindrance upon my business shall be broken now by the power of the blood of Jesus Christ.

6. I decree that I shall excel in everything I touch by the power of the blood of Jesus Christ.

7. I decree that the devouring spirits shall never be my portion in Jesus' name.

8. I decree that favor of God shall rain upon my life in Jesus' name.

9. I decree that favor of God shall rain upon my marriage in Jesus' name.

10. I decree that favor of God shall rain upon my business in Jesus' name.

11. I decree that favor of God shall rain upon my finances in Jesus' name.

12. I decree that every generation curse upon my life is broken right now by the power of the blood of Jesus Christ.

13. I decree that the spirits of dryness halt their activities over my life, and they are over by the power of the blood of Jesus Christ.

14. I break and paralyze every seed of barrenness upon my life in Jesus' name.

15. Every source of barrenness challenging my marriage dies in Jesus' name.

16. Jehovah Lord, arise with your mighty power and change every barrenness in my marriage to fruitfulness in Jesus' name.

17. I break every hidden curse of barrenness upon my life in Jesus' name.

18. Every witchcraft power nurturing barrenness against my life shall die in Jesus' name.

19. Every witchcraft power nurturing barrenness upon my marriage shall die in Jesus' name.

20. Every witchcraft power nurturing barrenness upon my business shall die in Jesus' name.

21. Every witchcraft power nurturing barrenness upon my finances shall die in Jesus' name.

22. Father Lord, keep my name in Your book of remembrance in Jesus' name.

23. Heavenly Father, change my situation around for good in Jesus' name.

24. Lord Jesus, let every curse issued against my home turn into blessings in Jesus' name.

25. Father Lord, destroy every evil designs fashioned against my womb in Jesus' name.

26. I withdraw my marriage from the hands of the wicked in Jesus' name.

27. Power of the night, release my marriage in Jesus' name.

28. I break every curse affecting my marriage negatively in Jesus' name.

29. Jehovah Lord restores all that the devil has stolen from my marriage in Jesus' name.
30. Heavenly Father heal all broken wounds in my marriage in Jesus' name.
31. I receive deliverance from barrenness designed by the devil over my life in Jesus' name.
32. I deliver myself from the hands of the wicked in Jesus' name.
33. Amen.

You must command the evil spirits to leave you.

You must continue to rebuke them *seven times* by the power of the blood of Jesus Christ, and they will leave you in Jesus' name.

You evil spirits that cause me to be bound to the attacks of barrenness in my marriage, I destroy you and all of your destroyers by the power of the blood of Jesus Christ, I renounce you and all your associate demons, and all your works in my life. I command you in the mighty name of Jesus Christ to lose your grip and release my marriage and me now by the thunder fire of God, in the matchless name of Jesus Christ I pray. Amen.

Chapter 26

Middle-Aged Marriage and Intimacy Issues

Middle-aged marriage intimacy and crisis issues are comprised of many forces that try to tear the marriage relationship apart. These cause intimacy in the relationship to wither and die. Many middle-aged people and senior adults experience serious issues in their sex life, and that can cause major damage in their marriages. As a man of God, I've received prayer requests from many men experiencing intimacy issues in their marriages, and their wives are not cooperative when it comes to intimacy.

This is an extremely sensitive topic to talk about, but many older people face this problem when it comes to sex within marriage. I have heard several complain similar to the comments below.

After their son was born twenty years ago: "I haven't had sex with my wife. Anytime I try to, she gets upset and starts calling me names."

Others say the last time they had sex was ten years ago.

"She has refused to have sex with me, and as a Christian man is it okay for me to have an affair outside my marriage?"

Some also ask if it's okay to divorce their wife if she has refused to have sex with him.

"My wife always gives me an excuse if it comes to sex, and I am really getting sick and tired of it. For the past five years, I haven't had sex with her; as a result of that, I've been married to spirit of masturbation. Pastor, is it okay for me to divorce my wife?"

I always respond to them no; you cannot divorce your wife as it is against the principles of God. Divorce is not an answer to your issue, but we can pray about it and ask God for his intervention into this situation. As the Bible tells us:

The husband must fulfill his duty to his wife, and likewise also the wife to her husband. The wife does not have authority over her own body, but the husband does; and likewise, also the husband does not have authority over his own body, but the wife does. - 1 Corinthians 7:3-4

I ask them, "Is your wife physically healthy? Is your wife having any disability issues that would restrain her from participating?" If all answers are no, then we proceed to pray to set the family free from any issues with the forces of the spiritual realm that may be blocking the family from experiencing a healthy sex life within their marriage.

As I have mentioned before, a spirit husband or a spirit wife who blocks them from normal, affectionate, and physical behavior has crippled some family members. These forces are beyond human control. Only deliverance can set them free from these evil attacks.

These attacks go both ways — either the husband or the wife is attacked. In many cases, too, the issue is the individual who is doing this from selfishness and pleasure seeking. That requires an intensive prayer to set them free to get back into reality away from spirit sexual encounters.

Why are many marriages falling apart today?

Why do many marriages suffer from sexual intimacy issues?

There are several reasons this happens.

The wife does not want to have sex anymore with the husband. Either she has no feelings whatsoever toward him, or no inclination for sex because of the way he treats her. Anytime the man asks to be intimate with her, she might give every excuse in the book not to have sex such as "my left toe is hurting," and "I don't feel like it today." Then tomorrow the wife says, "my right pinky hurts," or "Oh, you know what, I don't feel well," or "Oh, my nose and left eye itches, so I don't feel like it."

Husband love your wife as Christ loves the church. Many middle-aged and senior adult husbands never spend time hugging their wife, or kissing her! Some give excuses: "Oh, my wife is too boring," or "She's very slow in doing anything; I'm asleep when she finally gets to bed." The effort to begin making love to your wife in the morning for a pleasant night of love making at night is too much. They stop having sex with their wives. Instead, they are busy married to a spirit of masturbation or spirit of pornography, or running after younger girls.

If your wife is no longer attractive and thin as you used to know her fifty years ago, have you looked in the mirror lately? What do you think of yourself? Has your wife complained of how you look today?

These kinds of issues cause a high rate of divorce because when a woman always gives unnecessary excuses for not having intimacy with their husband, it usually forces the husband to look for love somewhere else.

Some women make all sorts of excuses when it comes to intimacy because they use it as a weapon against their spouse. If for any reason there is a financial hardship in the marriage or any disagreements about other issues in the marriage, the main weapon the wife will use against the spouse is refusing sex. This falls into a category of emotional abuse in any marriage.

There is an issue that sex is not confined to the marriage bed. Many people ignore the fact that God created sex for the pleasure of His people, husband and wife, so that both enjoy each other.

The word of the Lord tells us:

> *The husband must fulfill his duty to his wife, and likewise also the wife to her husband. The wife does not have authority over her own body, but the husband does; and likewise, also the husband does not have authority over his own body, but the wife does. - 1 Corinthians 7:3-4*

Wives, you must respect your husbands' feelings on an intimate level.

Wife, find a way in your relationship to please your husband because if you fail to do it, someone else will do it for you. Make a change or two in your appearance. Go to a salon and spice up your looks.

Husbands, respect and love your wives. Marriage is a trust between two parties. Focus on your wife and build a trustworthy relationship. If you want her to spruce up the house, teach her – or better yet, help her to do it. Education never ends.

Learn how to free yourself from the spirits of Jezebel, and concentrate on your wife. It takes a trustworthy man and woman to build up a healthy relationship in the home. Too many issues are invited into our homes, rather than jealously protecting the blessings that God has given the couple. Yes, everybody wants a loving home, a loving marriage; no one is going to do it for you. We must build that loving and trustworthy relationship and make our home a Christ-centered loving home.

> But seek first His Kingdom and His righteousness, and all these things will be added to you. – Matthew 6:33
>
> ...Walk worthy of the calling...with all humility and gentleness, with patience, showing tolerance for one another in love. – Ephesians 4:1b-2

Prayer

Everlasting Father, I dedicate my home into Your hands. I dedicate my marriage into Your hands. I dedicate my children into Your hands. I dedicate all that is around me into Your hands. I ask that You take absolute control over every department in my marriage. Heavenly Father, You know the ins and outs of my marriage, all the shortcomings, and difficulties. I ask for Your divine intervention. Bring my spouse and me together with much love and affection, heal my marriage where it needs healing, transform my marriage where it needs transformation, and deliver my marriage where it needs deliverance. In Jesus' mighty name, I pray. Amen.

1. Jehovah Lord, let the weapons of marriage intimacy used against my marriage collide with the Rock of Ages in Jesus' name.

2. Every spirit of controlling intimacy in my marriage catches the fire of God in Jesus' name.
3. Every spirit of pornography in my life breaks by fire of God.
4. Every spirit husband or spirit wife controlling my sex life burns to ashes by the thunder fire of God.
5. Every spirit against sexual intimacy controlling my spouse collides with the Rock of Ages and ground to powder in Jesus' name.
6. Any problem in my marriage that the agent of darkness has turned into an intimacy weapon against my sex life dies in Jesus' name.
7. Whatever situation that has caused my spouse to hold me in the sexual bondage of intimacy, blood of Jesus, take charge of that situation, and turn that issue into total blessings in Jesus' name.
8. Father Lord, renew the current of love in my marriage in Jesus' name.
9. Father Lord, increase the spice of love for my spouse in Jesus' name.
10. Jehovah Lord, destroy every evil rearrangement in my marriage in Jesus' name.
11. Sexual cravings and appetites for my spouse in my marriage, what are you waiting for? Back to work in Jesus' name.
12. Blood of Jesus, take charge of the sexual cravings of my spouse in Jesus' name.
13. Every spirit of gender manipulations controlling my life or my spouse's life breaks by fire of God.
14. Every spirit of gender confusion in my life or my spouse's life breaks by fire of God.
15. Every spirit of witchcraft activity in my life or my spouse's life breaks by fire of God.
16. Every spirit of barrenness in my life breaks by fire of God.
17. Every spirit of barrenness in my spouse's life breaks by fire of God.

18. Every evil spirit in charge of controlling sexual intimacy in my marriage dies in Jesus' name.
19. Every spirit of financial failure in my life breaks by fire of God.
20. Every spirit of infirmities in my spouse's and my lives holding us back from healthy sexual intimacy activities breaks by fire of God.
21. Every spirit of stagnancy upon my marriage breaks by fire of God.
22. Every spirit of frustration in my marriage breaks by fire of God.
23. Every spirit of anger and bitterness in my marriage breaks by fire of God.
24. Every devouring spirit in my marriage breaks by fire of God.
25. Every spirit of disgrace in my marriage breaks by fire of God.
26. Every spirit of embarrassment in my marriage, break by fire of God.
27. Every demonic curse upon my marriage breaks by fire of God.
28. I reverse every evil curse against my family and marriage in Jesus' name.
29. I deliver myself from the hands of the wicked in Jesus' name.
30. I deliver my spouse from the hands of the wicked in Jesus' name.
31. I deliver my marriage from the hands of the wicked in Jesus' name.
32. I deliver my providence from the hands of the strongman in Jesus' name.
33. Blood of Jesus, destroy every spirit of lateness fashioned against my marriage in Jesus' name.
34. Blood of Jesus, break every spell and enchantment programmed against me in Jesus' name.

35. Blood of Jesus, destroy every spirit marriage in my life in Jesus' name.

36. Blood of Jesus, destroy every spirit marriage in my spouse's life in Jesus' name.

37. Blood of Jesus, cancel every evil vow upon my life in Jesus' name.

38. Blood of Jesus, cancel every evil vow upon my spouse in Jesus' name.

39. I break and release myself from every evil marital curse in Jesus' name.

40. I break and release my spouse from every evil marital curse in Jesus' name.

41. Father Lord, let every family idol from both sides of my parents release my marriage and me by the power of the blood of Jesus Christ.

42. Father Lord, let every family idol from both sides of my spouse's parents release our marriage by the power of the blood of Jesus Christ.

43. I revoke every spiritual husband in my life in Jesus' name.

44. I revoke every spiritual wife in my life in Jesus' name.

45. I renounce every sexual sin that the devil has introduced into my life in Jesus' name.

46. I renounce all unholy covenants my forefathers have made upon my generation in Jesus' name.

47. I divorce myself completely from the spirit of sexual frustrations in Jesus' name.

48. I renounce all curses that I have brought upon myself, whether knowingly or unknowingly, through witchcraft and occult practices by the power of the blood of Jesus Christ.

49. Everlasting Redeemer, I thank You for answers to prayer in Jesus' name.

50. Amen.

You must command the evil spirits to leave you.

You must continue to rebuke them *seven times* by the power of the blood of Jesus Christ, and they will leave you in Jesus' name.

You evil spirits that cause me to be bound to the attacks of sexual intimacy frustrations in my marriage; I destroy you and all of your destroyers over my marriage by the power of the blood of Jesus Christ. I renounce you and all your associate demons, such as spirit of masturbation, spirit wife, spirit husband, spirit of pornography, spirit of bestiality, spirit of loneliness, spirit of drug addiction, spirit of alcoholism, spirits of anger and bitterness, and all your works in my life, I command you in the mighty name of Jesus Christ to lose your grip and release my marriage and me now by the thunder fire of God, in the matchless name of Jesus Christ I pray. Amen.

Chapter 27

Mood Swings

"I am lonely, yet I don't want to be bothered."

"Leave me alone. I don't want to be bothered."

"I have friends I can call, but I don't want them to know how I feel, and honestly, I don't want to pretend that everything is okay either."

"Honestly, I don't want to be bothered. Leave me alone."

"I get like this every now and then. It's as if I don't really know what I want."

"Do I really want to be alone?"

"On the other hand, I really don't want to be alone, and I really regret being alone, but I don't want to be bothered.

I know if you want to have friends, you have to pick up the phone and call them, but I don't want to know about anyone else's problems. I have my own to deal with. Yet, I am very lonely…but I don't want to be bothered."

"I really need human interactions in my life, but ever since my spouse died, I don't feel like being around anyone."

"Loneliness has become a trap in my life. I am always alone, feeling incredibly lonely, but I just don't want to be bothered."

"I can sense inside me that I am desperately in need of friends in my life. I really want friends because I am lonely, but I don't want to be bothered."

"Staying home alone all the time isn't an ideal solution. But for me, dealing with people is just too complicated, and sometimes I really get upset about it."

"Sometimes I'm really happy. Many times, I get really unhappy for no reason. I try to think of it as something hit me, and all I can see is that I am bleeding everywhere. I don't know what hit me. I'm full of loneliness, and I don't want to be bothered."

God Almighty knows that it is not good for man to live alone; therefore, He created both Adam and Eve.

> *Then the Lord God said, "It is not good for the man to be alone;*
> *I will make him a helper suitable for him."* – Genesis 2:18

God recognized Adam's need for contact with another human being. God created Eve. She was Adam's helpmeet, and whom he communicated with, shared ideas with, and loved and cherished.

If you are struggling with loneliness, you are not alone. Trust me; you are not the only one.

How is life treating you — are you winning or losing? I know life is not fair.

There are many young and elderly people who are isolated from other people. This kind of behavior is occurring more and more today, and doctors call it bipolar disorder.

In spiritual realms, there are demons in charge of such behaviors in human lives.

One spirit is called Loneliness, and this spirit travels with other spirits called Sadness, Evil Cry, Failure, Disappointment, and Frustration. Once any of these spirits gets hold of you, the rest come by default as they always travel together.

Their assignment is to destroy lives, as they are all demons of Satan, going about seeking whom they can devour.

The Bible tells us:

> *For our struggle is not against flesh and blood, but against the*
> *rulers, against the powers, against the world forces of this*
> *darkness, against the spiritual forces of wickedness in the*
> *heavenly places.* - Ephesians 6:12

Prayer

1. Powers of God destroy every spirit of loneliness in my life in Jesus' name.
2. Every soul-tie of spirits of depression in my life receives thunder fire of God Almighty.
3. Spirit of setback holding my life bondage loses its grip in my life in Jesus' name.
4. Whether consciously or subconsciously I'm trapped in the camp of Sadness, in Jesus' name Sadness burn up in the fire of God.
5. Spirits of failure attacking my life die in Jesus' name.
6. Spirits of disappointment attached to my providence break loose in Jesus' name.
7. Spirits of frustration bargaining for my life die in Jesus' name.
8. Spirits of evil attached to my providence catch the fire of God in Jesus' name.
9. Spirits of loneliness I am not your candidate; perish now in Jesus' name.
10. Every covenant of sadness and disappointments in my life, I break those vows in Jesus' name.
11. Every covenant of frustration and loneliness in my life, I break those vows in Jesus' name.
12. Every covenant of evil upon my life dies in Jesus' name.
13. Foundational bondage of loneliness over my life breaks loose in Jesus' name.
14. Every evil power had has demoted me into the camp of loneliness catch the fire of God in Jesus' name.
15. Be cancelled now in Jesus' name every incantation and ritual working against my life.
16. Every agreement of family idols over my life, over my spouse's life dies in Jesus' name.
17. Every agreement in which the spirits of loneliness hold my life bondage catches the fire of God in Jesus' name.
18. Heavenly Father, wherever the evil spirits have placed my providence, return it back to its original position in Jesus' name.

19. Yoke of loneliness upon my life breaks loose in Jesus' name.
20. Yoke of frustration upon my life breaks loose in Jesus' name.
21. Yoke of disappointments upon my life breaks loose in Jesus' name.
22. Yoke of evil cries upon my life breaks loose in Jesus' name.
23. Yoke of "I don't want to be bothered" upon my providence breaks loose in Jesus' name.
24. Yoke of "leave me alone" upon my providence breaks loose in Jesus' name.
25. Yoke of sadness upon my life breaks loose in Jesus' name.
26. Heavenly Father sends me a Godly spouse in Jesus' name.
27. Any powers inciting my divine partner against me catch the fire of God almighty in Jesus' precious name.
28. I shall be set free from the hands of the spirits of loneliness and aloneness whether my enemies like it or not in Jesus' name.
29. Jehovah Lord, I thank You for answering my prayer in Jesus' name.
30. Amen.

You must command the evil spirits to leave you.

You must continue to rebuke them *seven times* by the power of the blood of Jesus Christ, and they will leave you in Jesus' name.

You evil spirits that cause me to be bound to the attacks of loneliness, frustrations, sadness, disappointments, drug addiction, and from spirits of "I don't want to be bothered in my life," I destroy you and all of your destroyers over my life, by the power of the blood of Jesus Christ. I renounce you and all your associate demons; I command you in the mighty name of Jesus Christ to lose your grip and release my marriage and me now; by the thunder fire of God, in the matchless name of Jesus Christ I pray. Amen.

Chapter 28

Married but Single

If you have ever felt alone in your marriage, and said:

"I am married but filled with loneliness!"

"Married but single, I don't see any love left in my marriage! I was once happily married, but now the love is gone, and I am full of misery. My relationship has turned upside down; there is no more romance."

"My spouse does not want to have intimacy or any kind of romance any more. I am filled with loneliness in my marriage."

You are not alone.

There are many people who are married, but lonely. They live a single lifestyle at home. Their spouses do not speak to them unless they need something, such as a meal or sex; apart from that, there is no communication whatsoever within the marriage.

The wife controls the marriage and controls the husband, yet she comes and goes as she pleases. No respect whatsoever within the marriage. She engages in multiple affairs outside the marriage.

The husband lives with his wife, but treats her like an object, or as if she doesn't exist. He treats her like a housemaid. He controls her, beats her, and there is no love or intimacy within the marriage. He is always out with his friends, drinking and having multiple affairs with other females. He comes home when he pleases. There is no respect whatsoever within their marital home.

How do you break the cycle of abuse and loneliness in your marriage?

"I am married but I am lonely. I'm craving emotional intimacy with my spouse, but he doesn't seem to respond to anything I tried."

"I want to talk with her, but she isn't willing to listen."

If I ask, "How are you?" he responds, "Why do you ask?"

I ask, "Is anything wrong?" All I get is, "I don't want to talk about it," or "This isn't a good time to talk about this."

How many times have you heard these comments from your spouse?

They seem to indicate that someday, there actually will be a good time to talk, but that time never seems to come.

I wonder what went wrong in my marriage that makes me feel such loneliness and emptiness.

The emotional effects put me in an isolation stage, where loneliness leads to frustration, resentment, anger, bitterness, and sadness. I wonder if others feel the same as I do.

One must take the initiative in marriage. If you see yourself lonely, chances are your spouse is lonely as well. But her or she feels trapped in a cycle of emotional disconnect with a feeling of helplessness to break it.

Try to engage in conversations that are not about transactional details. Ask them for their opinion or views about something they like to do, then demonstrate you're listening. Do not expect them to change right away, as habits take time to change, but after a few gestures, they will return the favor.

For instance, if your spouse is in the other room alone watching their favorite show, join her — even though you can't stand the show they're watching. Start a conversation, and say, "I see you love this show, I want to give it a try." After the show is over, try and talk about the show and let her know what aspects of the show you like. Wives should make the same effort for their husbands.

You can suggest some activities such as taking a walk around the block, or in the park, cooking a meal together, and talks about things you both used to do. Make a smile a priority in your life, and learn how to be kind in all situations. The more upset your spouse gets, the more kindness you should provide in return. Fill him with kindness — I know it's not an easy thing to do, but it's the secret to a successful marriage.

Whenever you feel lonely and hopeless, remember that Christ Jesus is there with you. All you have to do is to call upon the name of the Lord Jesus Christ, as the word of the Lord assures us:

> ...And teaching them to observe all that I commanded you; and lo, I am with you always, even to the end of the age.
>
> — Matthew 28:20
>
> He will not allow your foot to slip; he who keeps you will not slumber. – Psalm 121:3

You should involve you and your spouse in healthy Christian fellowship. Let God take charge over your situation, and all shall be well with you in Jesus' name.

> With all prayer and petition pray at all times in the Spirit, and with this in view, be on the alert with all perseverance and petition for all the saints. – Ephesians 6:18
>
> The Lord is near to the brokenhearted and saves those who are crushed in spirit. – Psalm 34:18

Prayer

Father Lord, I am a sinner and I ask for forgiveness. Everlasting Redeemer, any sin in my life that would hinder my prayer of getting answered today, Lord Jesus, forgive me. Anyone I have sinned against that I do not know about, Lord Jesus, forgive me in Jesus' name.

Heavenly Father, your word declares it in the Isaiah that:

> "No weapon that is formed against you will prosper, and every tongue that accuses you in judgment you will condemn. This is the heritage of the servants of the Lord, and their vindication is from Me," declares the Lord. — Isaiah 54:17

1. Heavenly Father, I lift up my spouse who is lonely in our marriage.

2. I lift up the brokenhearted, those that feel unloved and unworthy. Lord Jesus, comfort them and grant them peace, love, and understanding in Jesus' name.
3. Everlasting Redeemer, give me thirst and hunger for my spouse.
4. I cast out every spirit of loneliness in my marriage in Jesus' name.
5. I bind and paralyze every spirit of setback and shame attacking my marriage in Jesus' name.
6. Fire of God destroys every spirit wife and spirit husband attacking my married life in Jesus' name.
7. I bind and break every unholy soul-tie against my marriage in Jesus' name.
8. Jehovah Lord, destroy every spirit of selfishness operating in my life in Jesus' name.
9. Every spirit of deception, spirit of rebellion, spirit of self-centeredness, spirit of "I don't want to be bothered," spirit of hopelessness, spirit of guilt, spirit of tension, and spirit of gender confusion attacking my marriage perish now by the thunder fire of God in Jesus' name.
10. Every stubborn demon that has refused to let go, and is attacking my marriage die without recognition in Jesus' name.
11. Jehovah Lord, cause both my spouse and me to cherish each other unconditionally.
12. Those who are in the middle of separation due to loneliness, our God, our Father, let your mighty fire reconcile them. Restore all broken marriages due to isolation and loneliness; fill that marriage with Your love, passion, and romance as well as love for each other in Jesus' name.
13. I soak every marriage that is in trouble with the blood of Jesus Christ.

14. I anoint all marriages with the Holy Spirit; I cast out every financial devourer and frustration within my marriage in Jesus' name.
15. Every agreement of spirit of loneliness holding my life in bondage catches the fire of God in Jesus' name.
16. Powers of the night pursuing my marriage die in Jesus' name.
17. Evil powers working on restructuring my marriage backfire by fire in Jesus' name.
18. Fire of God, burn every foundation altar over my marriage in Jesus' name.
19. Strange gods attacking my marriage perish now in Jesus' name.
20. Every enemy exploring a devastating strategy against my marriage collides with the Rock of Ages in Jesus' name.
21. Lord, perfect Your good work in my marriage.
22. Yoke of loneliness upon my life break loose in Jesus' name.
23. Yoke of frustration upon my life break loose in Jesus' name.
24. Yoke of disappointments upon my life break loose in Jesus' name.
25. Yoke of evil cries upon my life break loose in Jesus' name.
26. Yoke of "I don't want to be bothered" that is strangling my marriage break loose in Jesus' name.
27. Yoke of "leave me alone" strangling my marriage break loose in Jesus' name.
28. Blindfold all evil eyes, Lord, which monitor my marriage in Jesus' name I pray.
29. Thank you, Father God, for answered prayer. Thank you for sending peace and comfort like a warm blanket surrounding my marriage in Jesus' name.
30. Amen.

You must command the evil spirits to leave you.

You must continue to rebuke them *seven times* by the power of the blood of Jesus Christ, and they will leave you in Jesus' name.

You evil spirits that cause me to be bound to the attacks of married but single, spirits of loneliness, spirits of frustration, spirits of sadness, spirits of disappointment, spirit of drug addiction, and spirit of "I don't want to be bothered in my life," I destroy you and all of your destroyers attached to my life by the power of the blood of Jesus Christ. I renounce you and all your associate demons; I command you in the mighty name of Jesus Christ to lose your grip and release my marriage and me now by the thunder fire of God, in the matchless name of Jesus Christ I pray. Amen.

Chapter 29

Renew Your Marriage in a Godly Way

Marriage is for better and for worse. It's till death do us part.

Is your marriage built on a rock or on sand?

It's time to put Christ first in your marriage. Are you ready to live biblically in your marriage? Do you want a happy marriage or a miserable one?

When was the last time you experienced love and intimacy within your relationship with God Almighty? What about within your marriage?

Marriage is an intimate relationship. When a man and woman marry, God says they are one flesh. As Christian husband and Christian wife, they should also be of one mind. They pledge to be faithful to each other, kind, and loving to each other.

Dating couples often surprise each other with love notes, flowers, movie dates, going to parks, and dinner out. These thoughtful actions keep the romance alive. Try and set aside date nights with your spouse. Engage in fun and healthy activities.

Is your marriage Christ-centered? Honesty is a major factor in marriage. Are you honest with your spouse? Christians must keep the marriage bond strong, and one way is by praying together, which brings unity and intimacy into the marriage.

If we live God's way by making Him first in our lives, He then blesses our marriage, and is our provider with all the gifts and blessings He has planned for us.

How do we seek the love and intimacy of Christ? Here are promises of Christ on how to love and live healthily in our marriages.

Are not five sparrows sold for two cents? Yet not one of them is forgotten before God. Indeed, the very hairs of your head are all numbered. Do not fear; you are more valuable than many sparrows. – Luke 12:6-7

God is our refuge and strength, a very present help in trouble. Therefore, we will not fear, though the earth should change and though the mountains slip into the heart of the sea, though its waters roar and foam. Though the mountains quake at its swelling pride, there is a river whose streams make glad the city of God, the holy dwelling places of the Most High God is in the midst of her, she will not be moved; God will help her when morning dawns. The nations made an uproar, the kingdoms tottered; He raised His voice, the earth melted. The Lord of hosts is with us; the God of Jacob is our stronghold. – Psalm 46:1-7

For God so loved the world, that He gave His only begotten Son, that whoever believes in Him shall not perish, but have eternal life. – John 3:16

This I recall to my mind, therefore I have hope. The Lord's loving-kindness indeed never ceases, for His compassions never fail They are new every morning; great is Your faithfulness. The Lord is my portion, says my soul; therefore, I have hope in Him. – Lamentations 3:21-24

Finally, brethren, whatever is true, whatever is honorable, whatever is right, whatever is pure, whatever is lovely, whatever is of good repute, if there is any excellence and if anything worthy of praise, dwell on these things.

– Philippians 4:8

God wants you to respond to his love by trusting him.

Strategic Plan for Your Marriage

1. Show affection.
2. Let your attitude go. Get used to that.
3. Praise and encourage each other.

4. Do not use sexual intimacy as a weapon against each other; give sexual intimacy attention, as it can ruin your marriage if you hold back from providing it. Spend quality time on romance and intimacy.
5. Have a good relationship and friendship with your spouse. Learn how to be patient with each other.
6. Accept that in every marriage there is a little difference; do not let that spoil your relationship.
7. Build the marriage in spiritual growth.
8. Practice by spending quality time in Bible study, and praying with your spouse and family daily.
9. Allow God to be God in the center of your marriage.

Prayer

1. Father Lord, I thank You for making a way for my marriage in Jesus' name.
2. Everlasting Redeemer, I thank You for providing for my marriage in Jesus' name.
3. Heavenly Father, I thank You for peace and encouragement You have given my spouse in Jesus' name.
4. Christ Jesus, I thank You for the special grace You have brought over my marriage in Jesus' name.
5. The Father of the Fatherless, I thank You for all of the success You have given my family in Jesus' name.
6. Jehovah Yahweh, I thank You for the uncountable miracles, signs, and wonders over my marriage in Jesus' name.
7. The Alpha and Omega, place Your hedge of protection around my marriage and family in Jesus' name.
8. Omnipresent God, let there be an unusual outpouring of Your blessings upon my marriage and household in Jesus' name.
9. Abba Father, plead my cause this season and let my family arise in Your power, grace, and glory with

abundant over flowing favor and blessings in Jesus' name.

10. Jehovah-Nissi, scatter and put to flight every confidence of hell against my marriage in Jesus' name.
11. Jesus of Nazareth, remove every filthy garment covering my marriage in Jesus' name.
12. Everlasting Father, circle my marriage with Your thunder fire in Jesus' name.
13. Fire of God destroys anything ungodly in my family in Jesus' name.
14. Fire of God destroys every plan of the enemies over my marriage in Jesus' name.
15. God, destroy with holy fire every satanic strategy against my family in Jesus' name.
16. Fire of God take charge of everything upon my marriage and family in Jesus' name.
17. Thank You, Jesus for answers to prayer.
18. Amen.

You must command the evil spirits to leave you.

You must continue to rebuke them *seven times* by the power of the blood of Jesus Christ, and they will leave you in Jesus' name.

You evil spirits that have been causing problems here and there against my marriage and bargaining to dissolve my marriage, I destroy you and all of your destroyers over my marriage, by the power of the blood of Jesus Christ. I renounce you and all your associate demons, and all your works in my life; I command you in the mighty name of Jesus Christ to lose your grip and release my marriage and me now; by the thunder fire of God, in the matchless name of Jesus Christ I pray. Amen.

Chapter 30

Marriage is For Better and For Worse

Do you remember your wedding vows?

For better or for worse, in joy and in sorrow, in sickness and in health, as long as we both shall live—what a serious commitment we make in that moment, in front of God Almighty and all the witnesses around us.

A commitment is a mindset and an attitude that enables you and your spouse to go through the happiness and the storms of married and life.

Life is full of tempests. Many tend to fall out of the boat when the storm hits harder...

Your marriage requires greater determination, discipline, longsuffering during the storms so that you may enjoy the happiness and joy after the storms, or rather between them. Many things happen just because there are troubles common to man. Yet, God is faithful to provide the way of escape from any temptation.

No temptation has overtaken you except what is common to mankind. And God is faithful; he will not let you be tempted beyond what you can bear. But when you are tempted, he will also provide a way out so that you can endure it. - 1 Corinthians 10:13

Commitment is very important when the storms of financial ruin, storms of arguments, storms of disrespect, storms of unfaithfulness, and storms of disappointments hit. During this time of hardship, many tend to drop out of the journey. Once again, marriage is for better and for worse.

We are self-centered and stubborn.

Many of us today enter into a new marriage full of emotional baggage from our past experiences unable to forgive our past or others who have offended us. Filled with anger and bitterness toward God or others, we blame Him for our past. In truth, we have made some bad choices.

- We must learn how to forgive and forget, and let God take over all of our past. We must learn how to let go and let God in our marriages. A healthy marriage means to cherish each other, to love, to please, and to be submissive to each other.
- We must learn how to say I am sorry when we are wrong.
- We must cast into the pit of Hell the spirit of pride.
- We must cast into the pit the spirit of bitterness.
- We must cast out the spirit of abuse into the pit of Hell.
- We must learn how to restrain ourselves from spirits of unfaithfulness. Self-control is part of the Fruit of the Spirit.
- We must learn how restrain our bad behaviors.
- We must learn how to cast into the pit of Hell the neglect of love, affection, and intimacy.
- We must learn how to cast the spirits of no communication in our marriages into pit of Hell.
- We must cast away the spirit of "I don't care about your feelings" into the pit of Hell.
- We must cast out the spirits of "I will not give you any sex or intimacy" into the pit of Hell.
- We must learn how to compromise with each other.
- We must learn to embrace the tender mercies God has given us, and express tender mercies toward each other.
- We must learn how to enjoy each other's company.
- We must commit ourselves to Christ and allow him to take absolute control over our marriages.

   The husband must fulfill his duty to his wife, and likewise also the wife to her husband. The wife does not have authority over her own body, but the husband does; and likewise also the husband does not have authority over his own body, but the wife does. – 1 Corinthians 7:3-4

But seek first His Kingdom and His righteousness, and all these things will be added to you. – Matthew 6:33

Prayer

Everlasting Father, I put my marriage into Your hands. Any demons specializing in destroying marriages through abuse, unfaithfulness, pornography, sexual intimacy neglect make Your thunder fire strike these demons and burn them to ashes in Jesus' name.

1. Lord, make the weapons of marriage intimacy neglect used against my marriage by the spirits of marital problems perish in Jesus' name.
2. Every spirit of controlling intimacy in my marriage catches fire from God in Jesus' name.
3. Every spirit of pornography upon my life burns up by righteous fire from God.
4. Every spirit husband or spirit wife controlling my sex life and blocking me from having intimacy with my spouse burns to ashes by the thunder fire of God.
5. Every storm of issues challenging my marriage stills in peace by the breath of God Almighty in Jesus' name.
6. Every spirit of failure and disappointments upon my marriage grounds to powder in Jesus' name.
7. Any problem in my marriage that the agent of darkness has turned into an intimacy weapon against my sex life dies in Jesus' name.
8. Whatever situation that has caused my spouse to hold me in sexual bondage of intimacy, blood of Jesus take charge of that situation, and turn that issue into total blessings in Jesus' name.
9. Father Lord renews the current of love in my marriage in Jesus' name.

10. Father Lord destroys the spirits of pride in my marriage in Jesus' name.
11. Father Lord destroys every spirit of bitterness in my marriage in Jesus' name.
12. Jehovah Lord destroys every evil rearrangement in my marriage in Jesus' name.
13. Blood of Jesus casts every spirit of abusive marriage into the pit of hell in Jesus' name.
14. Every spirit of gender manipulations controlling my life or my spouse's life breaks by fire of God.
15. Father Lord destroys every spirit of marital unfaithfulness in my marriage in Jesus' name.
16. Father Lord, escort all demons in charge of marital frustrations and send them into the pit of hell in Jesus' name.
17. Father Lord, destroy every assignment of the spirits of bad behaviors in my marriage, and cast them into the pit of Hell in Jesus' name.
18. Father Lord, escort every spirit of "I don't care" destroying my marriage into the pit of hell in Jesus' name.
19. Every spirit of barrenness upon my spouse burns up by the fire of God.
20. Every evil spirit in charge of controlling sexual intimacy in my marriage dies in Jesus' name.
21. Every spirit of financial failure in my life causing all sorts of problems in my marriage dies by fire of God.
22. Every fountain of discomfort pouring into my marriage dries up now in Jesus' name.
23. Every spirit of stagnancy in my marriage breaks by fire of God.
24. Every spirit of frustration upon my marriage breaks by fire of God.
25. Every spirit of anger and bitterness in my marriage breaks by fire of God.

26. Every devouring spirit on my marriage breaks by fire of God.
27. Every spirit of disgrace upon my marriage breaks by fire of God.
28. Every spirit of embarrassment upon my marriage breaks by fire of God.
29. Every demonic curse upon my marriage breaks by fire of God.
30. I reverse every evil curse against my family and marriage in Jesus' name.
31. I deliver myself from the hands of the wicked in Jesus' name.
32. I deliver my spouse from the hands of the wicked in Jesus' name.
33. I deliver my marriage from the hands of the wicked in Jesus' name.
34. I deliver my destiny from the hands of the strongman in Jesus' name.
35. Father Lord destroys every spirit of lateness fashioned against my marriage in Jesus' name.
36. Heavenly Father breaks every spell and enchantment programmed against me in Jesus' name.
37. Amen.

You must command the evil spirits to leave you.

You must continue to rebuke them *seven times* by the power of the blood of Jesus Christ, and they will leave you in Jesus' name.

You evil spirits that cause me to be bound to the attacks of resentment, frustrations, and disappointments in my marriage, I destroy you and all of your destroyers over my marriage by the power of the blood of Jesus Christ. I renounce you and all your associate demons such as spirits of sexual neglect, spirit wife, spirit husband, spirits of pornography, spirits of shame, spirits of "I don't care", spirit of drug addiction, spirit of alcoholism, spirits of sadness, and all your works in my life I command you in the mighty name of Jesus Christ to lose your grip and release my marriage and me now by the thunder fire of God, in the matchless name of Jesus Christ I pray. Amen.

Chapter 31

Marriage Breakthroughs

Everyone deserves a marital breakthrough.

Whether your enemies like it or not, champion Christ and so shall your marriage be championed in Jesus' name. For marriages to be successful, each spouse must learn how to submit to one another, but most especially, how to submit to Christ. Jesus is the sustaining force in any marriage; after all, God created marriage. Solomon said that a person walking alone was easily overcome, two together can withstand an onslaught, and a three-stranded cord is not easily broken (Ecc. 4:12). When two are joined in holy love and matrimony, the Holy Spirit joins Himself with the two.

Satan has many tactics that he plays among couples, such as depriving one from the other. He infiltrates the mind with selfish thoughts that lead to selfish acts. Annoying each other, especially when there is a need for intimacy by saying, "No I don't feel like it," or by saying, "No I don't want any intimacy with you, I would rather watch porn movies," is especially selfish. These are the mind games that Satan plays. He is a master of deception on assignment to destroy happy families.

There are three main weapons that Satan usually uses to make sure there are no breakthroughs in the marriage such as weapon of addiction. Addiction comes in many forms and shapes. The major ones that Satan uses are sexual addictions, drug addictions, and alcohol addictions. These three issues have spoiled many healthy families.

One typical sign of an alcohol addiction is drinking alcohol first thing in the morning to recover from a hangover. Another sign is only going out to dinner at restaurants where alcohol is served.

Substance abuse and addictions do not just disappear. Rather they only get worse when left untreated. Substance abuse, which includes alcohol addiction, is a major source of family problems and marital breakups. It really affects all the members of the family, not just the one abusing alcohol.

Individuals with alcohol addictions have a distorted behavior. They will always justify their addiction from their family and friends — some frequent excuses are:

"Oh, I only drink once in a while just to cope with my family problems since my spouse is always nagging and complaining of everything."

"My job is too stressful."

"Children are always giving problems at home; that's why I always drink a little — it's just a release."

There is a spirit in charge of such behaviors of abusing alcohol. Their assignment is to make sure you crave alcohol or some chemical substance 24/7. They are out to destroy your life. Alcohol, like drug abuse, will kill you eventually.

You can attend many programs for treatments and all will be temporary — the longest will be two to four months, then you're back to your alcohol addiction stage. These are very wicked and destroying spirits whose assignment is kill and destroy happy homes and marriages. There are spiritual exercises such as deliverance one can follow to be set free.

There is another kind of addiction — drug addiction. There are demons in charge of drug addiction. These spirits of addiction are dreadfully powerful. Their claws sink deeply into your mind to destroy cognitive thoughts replacing them with cravings for the effects of the drugs. Once this spirit gets hold of you, he will make your life miserable; he will cause you to sell everything you have just to buy drugs. You cannot live with an abundance of some drug in your system.

Some drug abusers sometimes go as far as selling a family member for drugs. Some will prostitute their spouse or their child just to get drugs to use. For a person with a drug addiction, there is often a spouse who suffers from co-dependency. Co-dependent people have a great tendency to get involved with people who are unreliable, emotionally unavailable, or needy, and all they do is destroy everything around them including their families. These are the things that the spirits of drug abuse are good at doing.

> *The thief comes only to steal and kill and destroy; I came that they may have life, and have it abundantly.* – John 10:10

Just remember:

> *For our struggle is not against flesh and blood, but against the rulers, against the powers, against the world forces of this darkness, against the spiritual forces of wickedness in the heavenly places.* - Ephesians 6:12

The third addiction weapon Satan uses against happy families is sexual addiction. There are happy homes filled with Christ, but somehow one of the family members gets hooked by a spirit of sexual addiction. This spirit travels with many legions such as Pornography, Masturbation, Prostitution, Bestiality, Zoophilia, Sexual Perversion, and the spirit of Jezebel. Once Master Satan gets hold of you through any of these agents, they will make sure each one of these legions works on you spiritually and physically in different stages in your life.

The way around these kinds of problems in marriages is to equip yourself with the word of the Lord and prayer, and if you or your loved one has tangled with these agents of darkness, you must seek deliverance to cast these evil spells out from their life.

The word of the Lord tells us in Ephesians 6:10-24 that we should put on the full armor of God.

> *Finally, be strong in the Lord and in the strength of His might. Put on the full armor of God, so that you will be able to stand firm against the schemes of the devil. For our struggle is not against flesh and blood, but against the rulers, against the powers, against the world forces of this darkness, against the spiritual forces of wickedness in the heavenly places.*

Therefore, take up the full armor of God, so that you will be able to resist in the evil day, and having done everything, to stand firm. Stand firm therefore, having girded your loins with truth, and having put on the breastplate of righteousness, and having shod your feet with the preparation of the gospel of peace. In addition to all, taking up the shield of faith with which you will be able to extinguish all the flaming arrows of the evil one and take the helmet of salvation, and the sword of the Spirit, which is the word of God. With all prayer and petition, pray at all times in the Spirit, and with this in view, be on the alert with all perseverance and petition for all the saints. And pray on my behalf, that utterance may be given to me in the opening of my mouth, to make known with boldness the mystery of the gospel for which I am an ambassador in chains; that in proclaiming it I may speak boldly, as I ought to speak. But that you also may know about my circumstances, how I am doing, Tychicus, the beloved brother and faithful minister in the Lord; will make everything known to you. I have sent him to you for this very purpose, so that you may know about us, and that he may comfort your hearts. Peace be to the brethren, and love with faith, from God the Father and the Lord Jesus Christ. Grace be with all those who love our Lord Jesus Christ with incorruptible love. There are many promises of God that encourage us how to build successful marriages. – Ephesians 6:10-24

The husband must fulfill his duty to his wife, and likewise also the wife to her husband. The wife does not have authority over her own body, but the husband does; and likewise also the husband does not have authority over his own body, but the wife does. – 1 Corinthians 7:3-5

Stop depriving one another, except by agreement for a short time so that you may devote yourselves to prayer, and come together again so that Satan will not tempt you because of your lack of self-control.

Our help is in the name of the Lord, who made heaven and earth. – Psalm 124:8

Your sun will no longer set, nor will your moon wane; for you will have the Lord for an everlasting light, and the days of your mourning will be over. – Isaiah 60:20

How could one chase a thousand, and two put ten thousand to flight, unless their Rock had sold them, and the Lord had given them up? – Deuteronomy 32:30

Again I say to you, that if two of you agree on earth about anything that they may ask, it shall be done for them by my Father who is in Heaven. – Matthew 18:19

Prayer

Jesus of Nazareth, I glorify Your Holy name. Jehovah Lord, I magnify Your wonderful name. Heavenly Father, I just want to thank You, for You are God. The God of Shadrach, God of Meshach, and God of Abednego, I am here this moment to thank You for the marital breakthroughs You, Jehovah, have poured over my marriage. I adore You, Father. Glory be unto You. Thank You, Jesus, thank You, Lord, for all the marital blessings in Jesus' name. Amen.

1. Father Lord, pour out all marital blessings You created over my marriage in Jesus' name.
2. By the power of the blood of Jesus Christ, I unlock every closed door holding back blessings for my marriage in Jesus' name.
3. By the power of the blood of Jesus Christ, I release my marriage from the hands of the powers of the night in Jesus' name.
4. By the power of the blood of Jesus Christ, I release my marriage from the hands of the financial devourers in Jesus' name.
5. By the power of the blood of Jesus Christ, I release my marriage from every evil infirmity in Jesus' name.

6. By the power of the blood of Jesus Christ, I set my marriage free from the hands of the wicked in Jesus' name.

7. By the power of the blood of Jesus Christ, I claim happiness and joy to fill my marriage in Jesus' name.

8. By the power of the blood of Jesus Christ, I claim peace upon my marriage in Jesus' name.

9. By the power of the blood of Jesus Christ, I claim full understanding between my spouse and me in my marriage in Jesus' name.

10. By the power of the blood of Jesus Christ, I bind and cast out confusion and misunderstanding from my marriage in Jesus' name.

11. By the power of the blood of Jesus Christ, I filter out evil friends from my marriage in Jesus' name.

12. By the power of the blood of Jesus Christ, I bind and paralyze all false energy out of my marriage in Jesus' name.

13. By the power of the blood of Jesus Christ, I cancel out all evil strangers in my marriage in Jesus' name.

14. By the power of the blood of Jesus Christ, I invite Christ into the center of my marriage in Jesus' name.

15. By the power of the blood of Jesus Christ, Father Lord, let Your word overwhelm my spouse's life in Jesus' name.

16. By the power of the blood of Jesus Christ, Father Lord, let Your word overwhelm my marriage in Jesus' name.

17. By the power of the blood of Jesus Christ, Father Lord, let Your word take control, take charge over my children's lives in Jesus' name.

18. By the power of the blood of Jesus Christ, I send fire of God to destroy everything ungodly in my matrimonial home in Jesus' name.

19. By the power of the blood of Jesus Christ, I send fire of God to destroy any demons trying to make me doubt my God in Jesus' name.

20. By the power of the blood of Jesus Christ, I send confusion to the camp of my enemies in Jesus' name.
21. By the power of the blood of Jesus Christ, I send thunder fire of God to destroy every evil power bargaining for my marriage in Jesus' name.
22. By the power of the blood of Jesus Christ, I stomp upon lion and scorpions against my marriage in Jesus' name.
23. By the power of the blood of Jesus Christ, I claim the hand of God upon my family in Jesus' name.
24. By the power of the blood of Jesus Christ, I cast out evil hatred upon my marriage in Jesus' name.
25. By the power of the blood of Jesus Christ, I break every evil controlling spirit in my marriage in Jesus' name.
26. By the power of the blood of Jesus Christ, I cast out every stronghold rising against the peace in my marriage in Jesus' name.
27. By the power of the blood of Jesus Christ, I bind and paralyze every mind-controlling spirit challenging my life in Jesus' name.
28. By the power of the blood of Jesus Christ, I bind and paralyze every mind-controlling spirit challenging my spouse's life in Jesus' name.
29. By the power of the blood of Jesus Christ, I sentence every spirit husband and spirit wife upon my marriage into the Lake of Fire in Jesus' name.
30. By the power of the blood of Jesus Christ, I receive my marriage blessings in Jesus' name.
31. Heavenly Father, I thank You for Your divine blessings upon my marriage in Jesus' name.
32. Amen.

You must command the evil spirits to leave you.

You must continue to rebuke them *seven times* by the power of the blood of Jesus Christ, and they will leave you in Jesus' name.

You evil spirits that cause me to be bound to the attacks destroying my marriage, I destroy you and all of your destroyers by the power of the blood of Jesus Christ. I renounce you marriage destroyer, spirits of setbacks, spirits of marriage failure, spirit of sexual intimacy neglect, spirits of pornography, spirit of gender confusion, spirits of anger and bitterness, spirits of infirmities, and all your associate demons, and all your works in my life; I command you in the mighty name of Jesus Christ to lose your grip and release my marriage and me now by the thunder fire of God, in the matchless name of Jesus Christ I pray. Amen.

Chapter 32

Fruit of the Womb

Why are some married couples deprived of children?

What are the main causes of such an issue?

Children are gifts from God to married couples. It is His design for marriage and family.

It could be physical barrenness caused by medical problems such as ovulatory disorders, hormonal problems, malfunction of hypothalamus, or scarred ovaries that require medical attention. These problems cause women to be unable to conceive. If you have consulted your doctors, and no medical problems exist, then the problem may be spiritual in nature.

Some evil, spiritual attacks can be caused by evil spells and curses over marriage. By the power of the blood of Jesus Christ, whatever curse Satan and his demons have placed upon your marriage will be broken today in Jesus' name.

At the name of Jesus Christ, every knee shall bow.

Jesus has delivered me from the powers of darkness.

I am redeemed from the curse because Jesus Christ bore all sins.

Behold, children are a gift of the Lord, The fruit of the womb is a reward. – Psalm 127:3

And she cried out with a loud voice and said, "Blessed are you among women, and blessed is the fruit of your womb!"

– Luke 1:42

Prayer

1. Jesus of Nazareth, let my womb be purged by the thunder fire of God Almighty in Jesus' name.

2. I break every curse placed upon my womb in Jesus' name.
3. I cancel every evil vow over my marriage in Jesus' name.
4. Father Lord, touch my womb with Your healing hand, and destroy every evil infirmity in Jesus' name.
5. I command every work of the devil cease and desist in my marriage in Jesus' name.
6. I command all eaters of flesh against my womb to die in Jesus' name.
7. Anti-progress fashioned against my womb, be destroyed by the thunder fire of God in Jesus' name.
8. I withdraw my marriage from the hands of the oppressors in Jesus' name.
9. Father Lord, let every satanic spirit working against my womb woefully fail in Jesus' name.
10. Jehovah Lord, let the troublers of my marriage be troubled to death in Jesus' name.
11. I bind and paralyze all evil agent conspirators fashioned against the womb in Jesus' name.
12. Fire of God, take charge of every situation in my marriage in Jesus' name.
13. Father, remember my spouse and me like You remembered Rachel so she could bear Joseph, so that I shall bear children whether my enemies like it or not in Jesus' name.
14. I bind and paralyze every tree of sorrow and disappointments upon my marriage in Jesus' name.
15. I bind and paralyze every spirit of barrenness upon my life in Jesus' name.
16. I bind and paralyze every spirit of heaviness over my womb in Jesus' name.
17. I bind and paralyze every spirit of heaviness over my marriage in Jesus' name.
18. I bind and paralyze every spirit of bondage over my marriage in Jesus' name.

19. I bind and paralyze every spirit of disappointment over my marriage in Jesus' name.
20. I revoke every satanic decree upon my life in Jesus' name.
21. I revoke every evil decree upon my childlessness in Jesus' name.
22. I revoke every satanic decree upon my womb in Jesus' name.
23. I revoke every satanic decree upon my marriage in Jesus' name.
24. I revoke every satanic decree upon my body in Jesus' name.
25. I revoke every satanic decree upon my family in Jesus' name.
26. I shall laugh again whether my enemies like it or not in Jesus' name.
27. Every agreement made by my ancestors' demon-idols over my womb, be broken by the power of the blood of Jesus Christ.
28. Every agreement made by my ancestors' demon-idols causing spirit husband attacks in my life, be broken now in Jesus' name.
29. Every agreement made by my ancestors' demon-idols causing spirit wife attacks in my life breaks now in Jesus' name.
30. Every agreement made by my ancestors' demon-idols causing Incubus and Succubus attacks in my marriage be broken now in Jesus' name.
31. Father Lord, make all diviners powerless over my life in Jesus' name.
32. Every satanic checkpoint mounted against my marriage be scattered in Jesus' name.
33. I will not allow devourers to destroy the fruit of the womb in my life in Jesus' name.
34. I will not allow devourers to destroy the fruit of my marriage in Jesus' name.

35. I shall not allow devourers to destroy my family in Jesus' name.
36. I break every curse of embarrassment upon my marriage in Jesus' name.
37. I break every curse of disappointments in my marriage in Jesus' name.
38. I break every curse of failure upon my marriage in Jesus' name.
39. Heavenly Father, I thank You for deliverance of my womb in Jesus' name.
40. Amen.

You must command the evil spirits to leave you.

You must continue to rebuke them *seven times* by the power of the blood of Jesus Christ, and they will leave you in Jesus' name.

You evil spirits that cause me to be bound to the attacks on the fruit of the womb in my marriage, I destroy you and all of your destroyers by the power of the blood of Jesus Christ. I renounce you and all your associate demons and all your works in my life; I command you in the mighty name of Jesus Christ to lose your grip, and release my marriage and me now by the thunder fire of God, in the matchless name of Jesus Christ I pray. Amen.

Chapter 33

Let God be God in Your Life

Jesus said to him, I am the way, and the truth, and the life; no one comes to the Father but through Me. – John 14:6

For the wages of sin is death, but the free gift of God is eternal life in Christ Jesus our Lord. – Romans 6:23

For many are called, but few are chosen. – Matthew 22:14

We must make the right decision—don't satisfy Satan. Align yourself into God's truth.

There are many of us that act as if we know Jesus as our Savior, and pretend we are Christians, but deep inside we know we are not. It is just that we want to fit into the church society, be like everyone else. Since everyone around us is a Christian, we fake it so we'll be acknowledged and fit into the group. But, we haven't submitted our life to Christ to receive Him as our personal Savior and Lord.

How to accept Jesus Christ and be saved?

I pray that the mighty power of the Holy Spirit will pierce through your heart and bring you face to face with Christ. He is pleading on your behalf, and ready to accept you just as you are away from the bargaining of Satan and his demons. His great desire is to give you a new life. All who receive Christ, to them He gives the authority to become the children of God—those who believe in His name. Today is the day the good Lord has made for you to believe in Him, to receive his mighty power and the authority He has given us.

Everlasting Redeemer, I pray that You will help us with our unbeliefs. Let salvation be a part of our lives in Jesus' matchless name. Amen.

Jesus Christ is Our Father, who is waiting to save you. He saves everyone who will come to Him. When you believe that Jesus is the Son of God, and that He died for your sins, and when you are willing to accept Him as your God and Savior, you just need to pray for forgiveness and accept Him into your life. He will come into your heart, and make a new creation of new life.

If you truly believe and accept Him as your personal savior, you will be born again in the body of Christ and belong to Him forever. It will happen when you genuinely accept Jesus Christ as your savior and God. Let us pray for Salvation, and accept Jesus Christ into our lives.

So that at the name of Jesus every knee will bow, of those who are in Heaven and on Earth and under the Earth, and that every tongue will confess that Jesus Christ is Lord, to the glory of God the Father. – Philippians 2:10-11

Salvation Prayer

Father Lord, I am a sinner; I ask for forgiveness.

Any sin in my life that would hinder my prayer from being answered, Jehovah Lord, forgive me in Jesus' name.

Jesus, I believe that you bore all of my sins and died for me on the cross of Calvary.

Father Lord, wash away all my sins, and cleanse me with your Son's blood, the blood of Jesus Christ.

In Jesus' name, I pray Amen.

You are born again in the ways of Christ.

Once you have accepted Jesus Christ as your personal Savior and God, you have also given Him authority over your life. The best way of getting closer to our Father, and live Christ-like is to read the Holy Bible daily and pray with it.

Here are some helpful Bible passages to pray:

The Lord is my strength and song, and he has become my salvation; this is my God, and I will praise Him; my Father's God, and I will extol Him. – Exodus 15:2

The Lord is my rock and my fortress and my deliverer; my God, my rock, in whom I take refuge; my shield and the horn of my salvation, my stronghold. – Psalm 18:2

But the salvation of the righteous is from the Lord; He is their stronghold in time of trouble. – Psalm 37:39

But as for me, my prayer is to You, O Lord, at an acceptable time; O God, in the greatness of Your loving kindness, answer me with Your saving truth. – Psalm 69:13

By accepting Jesus Christ as your savor, you will turn your life in a better direction with Almighty God to live with Him not only here on earth but everlastingly in Heaven.

God Bless you for accepting Him as your personal savior and Lord.

About the Author

Dr. Davis A. Williams has a solid commitment to spread the Gospel throughout the world. He is founder and senior pastor of God Answers Prayer Ministries Inc., Feed The Needy Children Inc., Abused Women And Children, Inc., GAP Ministries Publishing Inc. These organizations work together to achieve his goal of spreading the Gospel around the globe.

He was born May 15, 1957 in Montego Bay, Jamaica, into a family deeply committed to ministry. He spent most of his childhood with his mother in West Africa Ghana, and then at the age of 14, his parents brought him to Los Angeles, California, United States.

Dr. Williams was sensitive to God's leading in his life, and felt God's calling at a very early age. Following in his father's footsteps, he became a minister. In 2006 in Van Nuys, California, Dr. Williams began God Answers Prayer Ministries Inc., and began travelling around the globe partnering with churches, and planting churches of God Answers Prayer Ministries through the worldwide project, Feed The Needy Children, Inc.

In addition to his evangelical schedule around the globe, Dr. Williams also finds time to fulfill another passion in his life, writing books. His books shine the light of truth in some hard-to-discuss issues. Some of the books he's written include *Marriage Destroyers, Altar of Addiction, Altar of Infirmity, Breaking Ancestral Curses, Household Wickedness, Heavenly Breakthroughs* and many more. The proceeds from book sales support God Answers Prayer Ministries, Feed The Needy Children Inc., and Abused Women and Children, Inc. His worldwide evangelism through a radio series blossomed because of his passion for people and his desire to reach the lost and broken souls.

As a dedicated family man, Dr. Williams attributes the support and encouragement of his wife, Edith Williams, as instrumental in helping establish God Answers Prayer Ministries. He and Edith have two children.

In 2002, Dr. Williams received a Bachelor of Science in computer science at UCLA. He went on to earn a Master's degree in theology from India Trinity Bible School of Apologetics & Theology Seminary in 2005. He completed additional graduate work for his doctorate in theology in 2007.

www.ingramcontent.com/pod-product-compliance
Lightning Source LLC
Chambersburg PA
CBHW051823090426
42736CB00011B/1628